VIDEO ICONS & VALUES

SUNY Series in the Philosophy of the Social Sciences
Lenore Langsdorf, Editor

and

SUNY Series, Human Communication Processes
Donald P. Cushman and Ted J. Smith, III, Editors

VIDEO ICONS & VALUES

Edited by

PN
1992.6
.V5
1991

Alan M. Olson,
Christopher Parr,
and Debra Parr

State University of New York Press

Published by
State University of New York Press, Albany

© 1991 State University of New York

For information, address State University of New York
Press, State University Plaza, Albany, N.Y., 12246

Library of Congress Cataloging-in-Publication Data

Video icons and values / edited by Alan M. Olson, Christopher Parr,
    and Debra Parr.
        p.   cm. — (SUNY series in the philosophy of the social
    sciences)
    Includes bibliographical references.
    ISBN 0-7914-0411-0. — ISBN 0-7914-0412-9 (pbk.)
    1. Television broadcasting—Influence—Congresses. 2. Television
broadcasting—Social aspects—Congresses. 3. Television
broadcasting—Psychological aspects—Congresses. I. Olson, Alan M.
II. Parr, Christopher, 1955-   . III. Parr, Debra, 1958-
IV. Series.
PN1992.6.V5 1991
302.23'45—dc20   89-49240
                                                                      CIP

10 9 8 7 6 5 4 3 2

Contents

Acknowledgments

This collection consists of the edited proceedings of a conference held at Boston University in 1987-88. "Video Icons & Values" was sponsored by the Department of Religion, College of Liberal Arts, and funded by the Humanities Foundation at Boston University.

In addition to thanking the principals, whose presentations are included herein, we also thank here the director and acting director of the Humanities Foundation, William Carroll and John T. Matthews, for their generous support of the project. We are also deeply grateful to the following moderators, panelists, and commentators who added so much to our proceedings: Professors Jean Berko Gleason, Leroy Rouner, Robert Neville, and Laurence Breiner, all of Boston University, and to Steven Brown, a producer of rock videos in London. Steven's incisive comments from "within" the industry, as it were, provided a grounding perspective when discussion became too remote or abstract. Hayden White, of the University of California–Santa Cruz, provided us with helpful counsel during the preparatory stages of this project, and Bob Riley, then Curator of Video at the Institute of Contemporary Art in Boston, and now Curator of Media at San Francisco Museum of Modern Art, served as an excellent guide during Dara Birnbaum's evening presentation of video art. Unfortunately, her work cannot be represented in this medium, nor can the multimedia presentations of Dick Hebdige and Gregor Goethals.

We are also deeply appreciative for the technical assistance extended to us by Media Services and the Geddes Language Laboratory at Boston University. Edna Newmark, from the University Professors' Program, generously extended her services in the transcription of much of this collection, and Debra Brown, of the Graphics and Publication Department at Boston University, provided us with some fine graphics. Finally, we extend our thanks to staff assistants Rosalie Carlson and Eric Helmer who attended to the many details inherent in a project such as this.

– 1 –

Video Icons & Values:
An Overview

Alan M. Olson

The broadcast industry recently celebrated 50 Years of Television, and the half-century mark is accurate, given the medium's commercial inception in 1939. Accounting, however, for a decade of disruption in the flow of consumer products during World War II and Korea, the time span is closer to 40 years. One would think that nearly a half century of virtual saturation by this medium should be sufficient to assess its cultural effects. Strangely enough, this does not seem to be the case; the values and disvalues of the medium remain as evasive as ever.

Perhaps one of the reasons for this imprecision has to do with the fact that the psychological disjunction between the world *before* and the world *after* television is so vast that critical issues regarding the nature and meaning of the medium are difficult to identify, much less address and resolve. Indeed, we are rapidly approaching a time in which there will be no living memory of a world before this medium; hence, we are not able to see the forest for the trees with respect to the task of criticism. We suspect that the criticism of culture generally rests on the criticism of television, so awesome and overwhelming is its power at the end of the twentieth century.

Thus while the industry congratulates itself on its amazing success story, others lament its vast intrusion into public and private life, an intrusion that not only has dramatically changed public and private values but that has itself become synonymous with the process by which values are formulated. Not surprisingly, this lamentation is particularly intense in academia where the conflict between book and video culture is most pronounced. In the past, when print held sway as the embodiment of high culture, such tensions were more containable by dint of being less visible. One could blissfully ignore low print culture, but video culture is another matter because it is everywhere. Hence scholars remain divided regarding the meaning and proper educational use, if any, of this medium. Such perplexity is informed by human interest, of course, as it is the bounden duty of academics, especially in the humanities, to preserve and, if possible, to extend the orbit of the classic by way of the print medium, which itself has enjoyed iconic status for about 5,000 years. We are, *pace* the prophet Muhammad, "people of the book" in more ways than one!

Many, perhaps most, intellectuals therefore tend to regard television with a certain disdain. And this disdain is easily vented in the case of television since, as the ever-present conduit of ready-made popular culture, it is the perfectly impassive object against which one may confidently direct one's contempt and derision without fear of backlash. Is it not true that television, even when viewed intermittently, instantly confirms one's sense of intellectual superiority? One thinks, for example, of the cartoonish image of a disgruntled viewer throwing an accessible projectile at a TV screen as if, by this emotive act, the power of the medium itself might thereby be negated. We are amused knowing that something analogous to this comic situation has probably happened many times. On second reflection, however, we may also be somewhat frightened in the realization that the indignant viewer will probably go out and buy a new and better video apparatus, indeed, feel compelled to do so. Thus we find ourselves in the somewhat curious situation where, on the one hand, intellectuals find it possible, even chic, to say nasty things about television anywhere, anytime, without fear of reprisal. One may even be congratulated for attacking something as allegedly banal as the pop culture television both spews out and stimulates with abandon. On the other hand, indignant critics of the medium will usually appear on television at a moment's notice if asked to do so. For in being popular culture's *raison d'être*, television is also identical with power.

TV-bashing, therefore, is a manifestly unconstructive and frequently dishonest activity, particularly in the academy where both the assets and liabilities of the medium and its messages have such far-reaching consequences. It used to be the case, in the earlier days of the medium, that conscientious parents willfully rejected television and banished it from the household, on the notion that its very presence would be deleterious to the educational development and overall mental health of their offspring. Some probably still do, but the valiant parents and individuals who eschew the medium by sheer acts of will are fewer and farther between. Video addiction today is a cultural fact, as evidenced by the recent appearance of bumper stickers enjoining us to "Just Say NO to Television" and as Marle Winn already observed in 1977.[1] It is highly unlikely, however, that any individual or group, private or governmental, can or even should be able to curtail the power and presence of the "electronic golden calf," as Gregor Goethals puts it (with a nod to Malcolm Muggeridge). Hence it behooves concerned individuals to investigate the nature and meaning of the new technological narcosis as carefully as possible. And if one is to deal critically and constructively with the matter of what we here term *video icons & values* one has to begin by acknowledging the video fact and then proceed to a consideration of the separate but interrelated questions of the nature of the medium and the messages purveyed through it. That is what the essays in this collection do by way of the theme of iconicity since, with respect to questions of value, it is of the very nature of an icon and the iconic to be nearly identical with what it means. A great deal of criticism, in fact, has been devoted to scrutinizing *what* the medium communicates; far less has been devoted to *how* this is done in terms of what television is as an instrument of consciousness and, in many ways, its substitute.

That such an inquiry is necessary should be evident from the now well-established fact that increasing numbers of undergraduate students simply do not enjoy reading very much any more. As a consequence, students nowadays do not know very much about the subject matter once considered to be a kind of baseline for entry-level college and university courses in the humanities. Invitations to "the adventure of reading," as library associations used to put it, seem now far more likely to be identified with "adventures in video." Obviously such a shift has tremendous educational implications, as it has been the traditional task of education to produce literacy and to facilitate what today is sometimes called "critical thinking" by way of intense involvement with printed texts. Such efforts become doubly difficult when students no longer regard serious, challenging reading as a pleasurable activity or even a labor of love but rather as a kind of drudgery to be endured and, if possible, to be minimized or avoided altogether. What critical thinking means in the absence of sustained exposure to the substantive content once identified with books is by no means clear. For if it is true that many students nowadays (students who have never known a time B.T., that is, "Before Television") have a tendency to regard the reading of books as some kind of unnatural act (which it probably once was, at least in the Rousseauean sense, and seems to be becoming once again), then we are certainly being confronted by a situation affecting not only the bookish professional denizens of academia but society as a whole.

It is precisely with respect to this larger social implication that the s ift from print to the video culture, as Jeremy Murray-Brown reminds , has something very basic to do with the growing and highly disturbing problem of aliteracy. There is mounting evidence, he points out, that increasing numbers of people today—even "educated" people—are simply disinclined to read even though they are entirely capable of doing so. This disinclination syndrome, fueling the problem of aliteracy, is precisely what makes it far more perplexing than the problem of illiteracy as such. One can do something about illiteracy, at least when illiteracy is viewed as a tactical rather than as a strategic problem: One targets those who need and who want help, and one marshals the necessary resources for the development and delivery of programs designed to improve necessary skills. People are thereby moved, at least statistically, into the ranks of the literate.

But aliteracy is the willful act of anti-literacy, whereby people decide that reading is no longer worth the time and trouble. And, as the evidence clearly shows, watching television is what people want to do the most. Indeed, viewing television is the activity most engaged in, Jeremy Murray-Brown reminds us, with the possible exceptions of sleeping and working. And, considering that many people are accustomed to sleeping with the television on, working with a television monitor joined with a computer or, given the growing ranks of the retired, not working at all, we must acknowledge that tremendous numbers of individuals are continuously in the presence of television. Given this astonishing scenario, the broadcast industry obviously has every reason to congratulate itself on a half-century of television, since within this modest temporal span the medium has moved from being an alternative presence in our lives (in the early days, it was a luxury that represented an investment equivalent to about 30% of the cost of a new car) to a presence now wholly

taken for granted. Many students, it seems, no longer pause even to consider the value or disvalue of including a television set with personal be-
longings as they move into their college residences; indeed, it seems far
more likely to be the case that students may ponder the feasibility of
"lugging" along a modest library—assuming that it is not a video library!

It is important to determine, then, whether the unconscious acceptance of television may not be rendering people unconscious, that is uncritical, in more insidious ways. In the recent, somewhat spirited, criticism of public education, however, little sustained attention has been
given to assessing the effects of television addiction on study habits and
academic achievement of students. Perhaps the issue has been avoided
since parents, by their own viewing habits, have already defaulted on the
matter of control. After all, such a line of critique implies that fault lies
more in the home and in culture generally than with teachers and
schools—the perennially convenient targets of an offended public, but
the "offended nature" of which usually lasts for about as long as they
have children in school. Former secretary of education, William
Bennett, softened the suspicion of television as the cause of low performance by reminding us that Japanese children watch as much if not
more television than American children. By this raw statistic we are to
conclude, it seems, that watching television is OK, as Japanese children
tend to be regarded as the global standard of academic achievement. But
by such resignation, we effectively relinquish responsibility for finding
out what precisely is going on when the offspring of an allegedly sapient
species have watched in excess of 30,000 hours of television by the time
they graduate from high school. Needless to say, passing over such an
astonishing statistic obviously absolves a very large, powerful, and largely
unregulated industry from accountability regarding the inculcation of values, whether by addiction to the form or the content of television or
both.

The problem of aliteracy, then, is exceedingly complex and involves much more than a mere skills adjustment, as both Lenore
Langsdorf and Renee Hobbs remind us in their essays. One of the most
consequential theoretical implications of our new state of affairs has to
do with recognizing that the vaunted reader-text relation (so long considered as being value-foundational by literate print-cultures) no longer is
fundamental to many people. What is increasingly fundamental is the
viewer-monitor relation as the primary and, for many, the only mode in
which information is received. Of course, it may be that what is viewed

on-screen is a text as is the case with word-processing on a computer. Even so, one still has to ask serious questions regarding the nature and meaning of this new kind of textuality and the effects of the video text on perception, consciousness, and value formation. What is happening, for example, when one begins to feel more comfortable with the soft video text than with so-called "hard copy" printed on paper? Does this mean that hard-copy is also becoming hard kinesthetically, that is, more difficult? If so, does such a shift signal changes in perception, changes in the act of cognition itself, that we are only beginning to understand? After all, many people in the past, even those who couldn't read, worshipped books simply because they were books. Some still do, unenlightened and enlightened individuals alike; in other words, some people are fundamentalists in the sense of being constitutionally incapable of distinguishing between medium and message. Is televangelism and the transition from bibliolatry to TV-olatry the harbinger of a new kind of fundamentalism in the wider kinesthetic sense?

Marshall McLuhan troubled greatly over such matters a quarter-century ago when the medium was relatively new and, by today's standards, still rather primitive. Yet it is very much in the spirit of McLuhan that Jeremy Murray-Brown explores, by way of his contemporary gloss on the Parmenidian and Cartesian *cogito ergo sum*, what he terms *video ergo sum* ("I view, therefore I am"). By this notion, Murray-Brown argues that the viewer-monitor relation signals a revolution at least as far-reaching in its implications and consequences as the previous revolutions in alphabetic writing and the mass production of printed texts. The respective axioms of Parmenides and Descartes, of course, were roughly contemporary with these earlier revolutions and probably presupposed the power of writing and printing. But if it is now the case that we are in the midst of a transition from writing and reading to recording and viewing as the primary evidence for the nature and quality of our existence, what does this mean with respect to the relationship between seeing and thinking? Are thinking and seeing related in more than an archaic metaphorical sense, seeing being a metaphor for understanding as it is in English and several languages? Is there such a thing as visual thinking, in Rudolf Arnheim's phrase,[2] and does it have anything to do with watching television, television being commonly regarded as a visual medium? Many artists, including some of those represented here, have their doubts; that is, many artists argue that neither the medium, given its technical limitations, nor its content, given the format of most commercial programming, can be regarded as being visual in the truly creative sense and may even be regarded as being anti-visual. How do we identify, Gregor Goethals asks, the kind of thinking that goes on both in the production and in the viewing of what is on television? To what sources of authority and value, Rebecca Abbott queries, is this medium actually transparent? The authorship of books is usually direct, but the authorship of television is highly anonymous. But if it is true, as Murray-Brown contends, that more and more viewers are of the a priori notion that what exists, exists on television, where is this new and increasingly axiomatic *video ergo sum* leading us?

Why, indeed, is it "so easy," as Renee Hobbs asks, to watch television? In order to answer this question one must, she argues, first obtain a better comprehension of the formal structures of the medium itself irrespective of any particular content that happens to be purveyed over or through it. The formal structure of the medium, she contends, constitutes both its power and its promise. Indeed, Hobbs's research demonstrates that even people who have never watched television before can instantly appreciate and comprehend highly complex formats. Thus she agrees with Murray-Brown's contention "that whatever television is, it is *sui generis*" and that the act of viewing both presupposes certain structural features of consciousness and also effects changes in consciousness with respect to value formation as one begins to view television habitually. Her position is not far from the view of Hans-Georg Gadamer who, arguing against instrumentalistic conceptions of language, asserts that "language uses us far more than we use it";[3] language, as a social reality, does not exist apart from specific contexts of mediation whether they be the context of living discourse, a printed text, or more complex technological contexts of the mass media. Hence we are faced with the task not only of understanding the functional properties of language conceived as an abstract system of signs, but of understanding how language works, as Lenore Langsdorf reminds us, within the specific life-worlds of culturally specific viewer-monitor relationships.

Like the other contributors to this volume, Renee Hobbs acknowledges the inevitability of television and its growing domination of the media—all media, even print. But this does not mean, she argues, that we have to accept the dominant commercial format of television, as resistant as it might be to change. She turns her attention to close scrutiny of the conventional formats in broadcast television. Her findings are fascinating since they suggest, on the one hand and given the sheer bulk of viewing time by the average American, that we are faced with a WYSWYW ("what you see is what you want") phenomenon. This, at least, is how the industry's quantity-based argument runs, namely, that if the viewing public were not basically satisfied with what is being broadcast, they wouldn't watch so much television as they do. But this argument, according to Hobbs, is based on the erroneous identification of content with format. In other words, while it may be that "what you see is what you want" is true with respect to content, it is not true with respect to format for the simple reason that commercial format has completely dominated television from its inception. Because most people don't know any other format, they don't seem to mind the subordination of content to the commercials that interrupt the flow of information every six to eight minutes in order to sell the products of sponsors. More disturbing is the realization that because the general viewing public does not expect any other format, because the public does not anticipate encountering any information that cannot be subsumed to this format, people begin to believe that *all* content can be contained within the three- or four-minute format. Needless to say, unconditional acceptance of conventional format strongly reinforces, and even renders normative, the fragmentation of meaning.

Hobbs's critical distinction between format and content also implies that the development of a critical consciousness is not, as some contend, precluded by the medium itself. In her view, the development of critical consciousness is precluded only by the conventional format that presently dominates broadcast television; a format which, while providing tremendous variety, provides little or no diversity. Network television is unwilling to experiment with format as such experimentations will result in reduced revenues through the loss of market share. There is little incentive to have it any other way, the economic motive being rather to keep things the way they are. If one really insists upon diversity, one pays for cable or one pays extra for additional channel subscriptions but even then, with some 50-100 channels, there is still very little diversity.

It might then seem, Hobbs muses, that there is little we can do about this situation given the fact that most people, owing to their habituation to conventional format, simply will not look very long at experimental television ("television that makes you think," as she puts it). This problem is documented rather dramatically in Rebecca Abbott's account of the commercialized domestication of "Max Headroom" by network television. The American adaptation of this British program is a classic case, Abbott contends, of what critical theorists such as Adorno, Horkheimer, and Marcuse have described as the dialectical inversion and sublation of anti-establishment cultural forms by dominant, establishment cultural media. Other aspects of the same problem are developed at length in David Thorp's imaginative meditation on engravings by Albrecht Dürer wherein Melencolia is depicted as a pioneering video artist having neither the confidence of the political Knight nor the serenity of the religious Saint (lacking the support of both state and church). Hence the video artist finds himself or herself increasingly consigned to the status of a computer peripheral or, given the dominant commercial format, to the status of the commercial peripheral, the function of which is to provide more zip for the sales pitch so that it won't be zapped by the now-standard remote control. We are so conditioned by the prevailing commercial format, Hobbs argues, that we resist all changes in the way material is presented; and because we resist changes in the presentation of material or in format, we resist any changes in the viewer-monitor relationship—especially changes in the way we see things, which might demand movement from being a merely passive or uncritical viewer to becoming an active or critical one.

If we are concerned, however, about making television and video into a more productive cultural and educational instrument, that is, if we are concerned about the development of a critical consciousness through rather than in spite of the viewer-monitor relationship that increasingly dominates our lives, then changes in format must be encouraged and made. Some would argue that technological advances (especially the advent of HDTV and/or fiber-optics telecommunications) will automatically bring about innovations in format; others are not so optimistic, believing that the tail will continue to wag the dog, so to speak, as long as the medium remains almost entirely commercial. An unregulated or deregulated industry, skeptics argue, means that it remains regulated *de facto* by strictly marketshare considerations, hence dominated by commercial format.

Our contributors are largely agreed that the primary critical-cognitive consequence of the dominant conventional format, is the fragmentation of meaning that results from a steady diet of television viewing. More specifically, this fragmentation of meaning follows as the inevitable consequence of what Neil Postman has identified as the " . . . and now this . . . " syndrome in which the conjunction *and* effectively functions, in conventional broadcast television, as a disjunction or the *disconjunc-tion* that interrupts the stream of information bits which are the fodder of commercial television.[4] For by the editorial use of the " . . . and now this . . . " disconjunction (whether spoken by an announcer or unspo-ken in the automatic commercial pause) practically all information, whether important or unimportant, sublime or ridiculous, consequential or trivial, is conveyed in the 30-60-second snippet with little, if any, log-ical connection between snippets. And while it may be the case that cer-tain sequences of snippets contain some modest rational judgment, the values implicit in such judgments are entirely subordinate to a superven-ing editorial logic regarding the necessary patterns of commercial mes-sages. Thus the viewer may, at one moment, find him or herself startled by the horrendous news of a major airline disaster, and in the very next moment be confronted by an airline commercial enjoining us to "fly away" to some island paradise. And since there may be as many cuts or edit points in the slick, incredibly expensive commercial as there are sec-onds of broadcast, such *non sequiturs* are usually far superior aesthetically to what is shown between them. In such situations, one may discover that many, especially children, are captured more by the alleged reality of the commercial than what is being reported, the consequence being that the actual world becomes, in contrast to commercials, rather boring.

To have it any other way would negate the purpose of commercial format; but to have it the way it is virtually guarantees the fragmentation of meaning. It is rare when a major network suspends the " . . . and now this . . . " fragmentation syndrome in order to provide live, sus-tained coverage without commentary or further interruption. Nor is there ever a time, during the live coverage of a sporting event, a political convention, or a congressional hearing ("C-Span" being a notable excep-tion), when one is ever free of a continuous voice-over by some allegedly omniscient commentator telling the viewer what to think about what he or she is seeing. In fact, the primary function of the voice-over is not to provide authoritative or insightful commentary but rather to convey an illusory community for the otherwise solitary viewer. Such a function is best served by sticking with the voice-overs of celebrities whom viewers think they know and like to have in their homes. To recruit individuals with intellectual incisiveness on a given topic would make the average person uneasy and many intellectuals are frequently difficult to control. It goes without saying that commercial television, as Hobbs, Abbott, and Goethals indicate, is itself very uneasy when it fails to control the meaning of what is being broadcast since failures to do so may have drastic economic consequences. But exercising this control, whether by the tried-and-true celebrity intellectual on live broadcasting, or by the routine commercial editing of "non news" broadcasting and LOP ("least objectionable programming"), obviously fosters and promotes the illusion that *all* the meanings and values worth having are immediate and can be paced, so to speak, as easily as the selling of hamburgers and toothpaste.

Is it any wonder, then, that so many students, after eighteen years of continuous habituation to this kind of fragmentation, should develop a kind of K-byte consciousness or mentality that seems able to tolerate no more than a few minutes of focused attention and concentration? Is it any wonder that after being continuously wired for the commercial sounds of the local rock-and-roll music station students should find it difficult to follow an argument that lasts longer than three minutes? Lenore Langsdorf thinks it is not surprising at all and attributes the inability of many students to recognize and develop any kind of sustained argument in what they read and write directly to the domination of consciousness by the mass media. The critical analysis of information by way of discernment and sustained evaluation simply cannot be accomplished, she argues, by a mind entirely conditioned by the discontinuous 30-second-information-bit. Continuous bombardment by such bits, in fact, negates altogether the possibility of sustained critical reflection. It might be argued, somewhat ironically, that as major sections of the SAT and GRE are also modeled on the disjunctive information bit, they also encourage this process of fractionation. Software designers are increasingly adept nowadays at showing how one can beat such instruments by teaching students to process information more effectively in order to avoid getting stuck with problems of comprehension, since too much attention to comprehension will "slow you down!"

The effect of the " . . . and now this . . . " fragmentation syndrome, then, seems to be direct encouragement of the diastatic, disjointed consciousness in which people are taught, as Hobbs puts it, to encode certain kinds of information for which they have preexisting schemas (e.g., health, sports, entertainment, etc.), and to overlook or ignore data for which they have none (e.g., international affairs, geography, economics, philosophy, science, art, etc.). One obtains schemata for the former mundane type of information simply by being a sentient consumer. But complex schemata cannot be provided simply by being a consumer—at least not by being an ordinary consumer. Again, it is not that television, by its very nature, is incapable of being used to develop critical schemata. It is rather the case that commercial television chooses not to do so for strictly economic reasons. Hence critical schemas of the type prized in higher education have to be obtained elsewhere. But the obtaining of such schemas—geographic knowledge, for example, or philosophy and politics—is virtually impossible for people who will not spend some considerable time with books or with "life" in the larger sense. And since reading, as mentioned previously, is no longer identified by many as an immediately pleasurable activity but with the slow *work* of critical mediation and reflection, it is not readily evident, given the influence of popular television, how this situation can be improved.

It seems reasonable to conclude with Lenore Langsdorf, then, that the disjunctive, fragmentary, conventional format which dominates broadcast television is a major contributing factor in what she identifies as the inability of many students to see any difference between explanatory and interpretive modes of understanding. Langsdorf develops this distinction by way of pointing out that many students fail to discern any difference between an author's opinions and the text's position as that position has been developed through an argument. While the notion that "everyone's entitled to his/her own opinion" may signal what some might regard as the definitive rise of value egalitarianism, she thinks that this is highly unlikely. A more plausible explanation, given the utilization of opinion polls *ad nauseum* as indices of reality, follows from what she identifies as the *linearnarrative* character of most programming on the mass media. This is evidenced, she points out, by the almost exclusive reliance on simple plots in sitcoms, soaps, action dramas and the even more simplified and/or compressed linear plots in ads and news stories organized, as they are, by what Jeremy Murray-Brown refers to as the "conflict-resolution" model of meaning and value. The simple linear plot is made necessary, of course, by the conventional, commercial format in which the meaning of the message must come across within eight minutes or, in the case of commercials, within 30 seconds. But these format-imposed temporal constraints obviously preclude, Langsdorf argues, the possibility of nonlinear, noncausal analyses of the meaning of what is being broadcast, as viewers always expect automatic resolutions of meaning in the conclusion. Obviously this configuration of format and content means that it is virtually impossible for the viewer to encounter, much less consider, the meaning of values that are critical or transcendental (except, perhaps, on PBS). But lest we take comfort in the availability of educational television, we are reminded by Renee Hobbs that only about 5-10% of the viewing public ever come into any kind of sustained contact with noncommercial broadcasting. Indeed, educational or public stations have themselves been forced to emulate commercial networks in order to attract viewers and sustain contributors.

Langsdorf is not saying that it is possible to develop transcendental values, critical values, only by way of print media. Her argument is informed, rather, by distinctions having to do with the kind of critical mediation most likely to occur in print versus video media. In short, there is a basic difference between *mediated* experiences which are controlled altogether in terms of being designed as vicarious substitutes for actual experiences, and those experiences that may be termed *lived* or that encourage one to go beyond the agent of mediation. While video experience, like all experience, is lived, there is a fundamental difference between experiencing what is being presented and/or represented by way of second- and third-order mediations (whether in word or image), and the actual experience of what is being mediated. Hence we are forced to confront the larger question having to do with the nature and meaning of what might be termed the new *media dependency* and whether this dependency may not be altering the focal plane of consciousness in such a way that mediation-in-itself becomes a substitute for actual experience, especially for critical questions of whether a given mediation is accurate and therefore true. Such questions force one "beyond" the medium. The cynical adage, "Don't believe what you read in the newspapers," simply does not extend, for most people, to what one "sees on television." One of the more astonishing examples of this, as Murray-Brown indicates, is the growing number of individuals who rent travel videos as a substitute for actually taking the trip.

If it is the case that transcendental values or values of critical substance are best developed in and through lived experience, does this mean that young people in our hypermediated culture are necessarily bereft of such values? Without having a clear answer to this question, Langsdorf has suspicions regarding reliance on the increasingly dominant viewer-monitor relation since it minimizes, far more than the reader-text relation, the need for lived experience in the more immediate sense. The concept of lived experience today, given the domination of video, has the character of being a substitute for all experience, given the tendency of viewers to conclude that everything is like everything else simply because we have instant access to everything—just like on television.

There is every reason to believe, however, that this hypermediated, wired world will become ever more mediated and wired as time goes by. The truly challenging questions facing us have to do with the creative and constructive educational use of this technology, realizing that we can ignore its power only at our own risk. Several of our contributors, especially those with sustained visual media experience, provide creative and challenging indications as to how this might be accomplished or how, at the very least, we might begin to regard video technology as the servant rather than the master of meaning. Robert Scholes's new theory of rhetoric is especially germane in this regard as it is a theory expressly aimed at the analysis and critique of the videos (whether entertainment or commercial videos) that dominate all aspects of popular culture. Such a theory of rhetoric, he explains, is quite different from the views we find expressed in Plato, Aristotle, and the "modernist inheritors of Romanticism" such as Yeats and Joyce. In these cases, he argues, we have a theory of rhetoric informed by what he terms the binary opposites of popular or *low* art, on the one hand, and literary *high* art, on the other. This distinction originates, he believes, in the semi-dualistic configuration of traditional virtues such as action and contemplation, the impure and the pure, of persuasion versus truth. Given the gradual erosion of these oppositions in the modern world, it has been the tendency of the modernist to contemplate the pure aesthetic object as the substitute for knowledge of the allegedly discredited metaphysical and/or supernatural truths of philosophy and religion. Alas, this aesthetical remainder is inadequate for all except the aesthete because, as Hegel was one of the first to observe, "while Enlightenment has the power to empty the wine-skins of belief, it has nothing new to substitute."[5] As such, the romantic-modernist view of aesthetics might be viewed, it seems, as the final stage in the secular denouncement of the post-Enlightenment pietistic, anikonic religious traditions of the West: These traditions, Dick Hebdige indicates, hold the notion that "God can be apprehended only through the Word" and not through the image. But with the absence of external reference, only subjective feeling remains, and it is feeling doomed to remain subjective apart from any agreement regarding value or, as in Alasdair MacIntyre's view, any consensus regarding the nature of virtue.[6] Hence it tends to be assumed (perhaps today more than ever, given the tensions between print and video culture), that rhetoric, as Scholes puts it quoting Aristotle, is uniquely suited to "those who cannot follow a long chain of reasoning" (namely, television viewers) and who, therefore, rely on the emotions (namely, visual immediacy) from which values and/or disvalues follow willy-nilly.

Nevertheless, Scholes argues that this distinction is informed, at bottom, by a false distinction between high and low culture, and that we must begin to recognize that the difference between the world of television and the world of books is one of degree rather than kind. To this end, he commences the task of developing his new theory of rhetoric by way of the notion of *textual economy,* a notion broad enough to include all sorts of texts including video texts, yet narrow enough to address basic questions of value.[7] Within his notion of textual economy, exchanges of value take place with texts as the media of transfer. In textual economies as in markets of exchange generally, we are dealing with the purchase of something with power for the sake of pleasurable consumption. In such transactions one "surrenders" for a moment, as Scholes cites T.S. Eliot, to the medium of exchange, that is, surrenders to the text. The second and really decisive moment in this transaction, of course, is what he terms "recovery" from this surrender; a recovery that involves or, more accurately, depends upon distantiation whereby one can critically evaluate the "beliefs" one has, in the first moment, entertained.

But from where does one receive the power of "critical distantiation," especially if one's sole source of information is the television video? This is a hotly debated issue and another aspect of the questions raised by Langsdorf. On the one hand there are those who would contend that the power of critical response can only come by way of the printed text (namely, that the "pause" button on one's VCR is not the same as "pausing" to consider the meaning of print), especially the celebrated, canonical texts of high culture. This is the case for the continuation of the classical critical education against whatever odds. Others, like Hobbs, Scholes, and Goethals, take issue with this position: Hobbs by way of arguing that it is a position that presupposes a specific kind of format convention in television; Scholes by way of arguing that the advocates of traditional, classical print-culture tend to overlook differences in the way people actually live their lives, that is, tend to disregard the values and virtues already present in the lives of ordinary folk; and Goethals by her analysis of the mythic structures of ordinary television narratives.[8] The disregard Scholes alerts us to may be informed by a cultural elitism that simply refuses to recognize the positive values that have developed as the result of mass communication. Nevertheless, such values are present, Scholes and Goethals argue, in the universally human ability to share the simple aesthetic pleasures of a commercial or sitcom by way of bearing witness to the fact that we are, in fact, alike at deeper levels of meaning and value. And it is a likeness or similarity both formal and material: By paying attention to the images of popular culture, we begin to discover how commercials and videos with iconic or near-iconic status both depend upon and articulate in extremely powerful ways the complex structure of the basic human values they presuppose. In this regard the rhetorical processes informing the operations of television production are no different, Scholes argues, from the processes through which great poets, such as Sophocles and Aeschylus, produced their tragic plays. In both instances, successful production depends upon having creative access to the values the viewers of such productions already possess, to the structures of particular life-worlds, and to the symbolical and valuational elements whereby a given narrative makes sense.

This is why today's videos must be taken seriously and why, according to Scholes, the criticism of videos must be taught in school. After all, it has been the case in print-culture for generations that the task of educators is not merely to get students to read, but to read and appreciate certain books: the so-called Great Books. It follows, then, that central to the task of educators responsive to today's video-culture is the fashioning of an interactive hermeneutics of the video text—a task no more or less difficult than a hermeneutics of the conventional text.

Without question, the present revolution in central and eastern Europe should provide impetus to this challenge. There are many who argue that this revolution, especially its speed and momentum, is fueled by Western television more than any other single medium of communication. While we do not, in this volume, deal directly with this phenomenon, the issues raised with respect to the meaning of video icons & values in the larger international setting clearly suggests another stage of research and, indeed, a sequel to the present study.

– 2 –

Video Ergo Sum

Jeremy Murray-Brown

A person born in 1453, the year that Constantinople fell to the Turks, if he lived to be 50, would have seen more books produced in his lifetime—some eight million—than had been written in the previous thousand years of Constantinople's existence.[1] This is how Elizabeth Eisenstein dramatizes in quantitative terms the revolution in communication brought about by the printing press. The print revolution, she argues, worked a radical transformation in Christendom that led, among other things, to the rise of western science, the Protestant Reformation, the voyages of discovery that gave Europe the mastery of the globe, the introduction of assembly-line production, and the idealization of Italian Renaissance art. In short, a revolution in the technology of communication was responsible for our civilization in matters of science, religion, art and politics.

Some 50 years have now passed since the first public transmission of a commercial television program. And in these 50 years, what an extraordinary advance television has made across the cultural landscape! In the United States no major city is without competing television stations, very few homes are without a television set, many have several, three-quarters of them can choose among more than ten channels, almost half are linked by cable. We are now in the same position in relation to this new medium of communication as was our 50-year-old born in

1453. No one can doubt that there has been an advance in the technology of communication. But can we discern the full consequences of this advance?

It seems to me that television has indeed turned out to be the agent of a radical change in human consciousness, comparable to the revolutions in communication that occurred with the invention of alphabetic writing and print. I use the term *human consciousness* in the manner defined by Walter Ong as "the individual's own sense of presence in and to himself and in and to the world around him."[2] I acknowledge that I have been much helped by the work of Ong and others on the dynamics of change in human consciousness brought about by earlier changes in the technology of communication. It is significant that studies in these earlier revolutions in communication history are of recent appearance, prompted in fact by the momentous nature of the television revolution. It is only because of what has happened with television that we have begun to understand the specific cultural and psychological ramifications of oral expression, writing, and print.[3]

In the case of television, I shall not spend time discussing the question of evolution versus revolution, interesting though this question is. The influence of photography, film and radio, the tradition of the circus, the vaudeville, the theater, a general surge of technological inventiveness, and many other factors have gone into making television what it is. But what it is, it is *sui generis*.

Much criticism can no doubt be leveled at the commercial nature of American television, at the pressure of advertising that spurs networks to seek the biggest possible audience in order to increase ratings and maximize profits. But it is these commercial incentives that have enabled television to exploit the costly technology that has made it a truly popular mass medium. A fundamental psychological characteristic of television viewers is the desire to watch of their own free choice what everyone else is also watching. It is only through the free market process that this desire can be met, although the British 1986 report on the financing of the BBC, the Peacock Report, takes a somewhat different line on this subject.[4] Ninety-five percent of Americans, however, choose to watch commercial television,[5] and many would argue that television in America is television in its most natural state.[6] I believe myself that the American model is destined to be followed, eventually, everywhere in the world.

Let us then first look at this cultural phenomenon we call television. I come at once to a startling figure: In the western world today (I include Japan) people are spending between a third and a fifth of their waking lives watching television. The statistics, of course, are imprecise and open to debate, but the main point is clear enough. In Japan, in North America, in northern Europe, what is significant about television is not the vast audience for this or that program, impressive though these audience sizes are, especially if it's a royal wedding or a World Cup final. No, what is significant is the total amount of viewing that most people subject themselves to, day in and day out, morning, noon, and night, for most of their lives. In the average American home, the television set will be switched on for more than six hours a day; in Japan, for more than eight hours;[7] in Britain, for at least five. In the United States, first graders will spend the equivalent of one entire 24-hour day per week watching television, more time than they spend in the classroom. For most people in the United States, viewing television has become the third most common activity after sleep and work.[8]

This quantitative appraisal of the television revolution must be set alongside the facts about illiteracy (although these facts, too, are hotly debated); for example, something in excess of 60 million Americans are wholly or functionally illiterate.[9] That is to say, something like 40% of the voting population of the United States is unable to participate in any form of communication that depends on literary convention. And then there is *aliteracy*, the capacity to read but disinclination to do so, estimated by the outgoing Librarian of Congress to represent about 44% of the adult population.[10]

Many of us are shocked by these figures, but they are overwhelming in their reality. Because of them and what they imply, there is, in my view, little point in discussing external controls. The world wants television, and the world is going to get it. Our culture is changed, changed utterly.

For television is much more than an optional activity; rather, it has become a necessary component of all of life's activities, public and private, and its influence is evident in a thousand different ways. Instead of suicide notes we have public figures blowing their heads off in front of the cameras, and instead of a letter to the newspaper we have a man barging into the television studio with a handgun demanding that his statement be delivered live over the air. Television has invaded territory far from the living room: witness its increasing use in courtrooms, or as evidence of authentic personality, as in the Bernard Goetz trial. We now hear of videotapes for use on VCR machines that enable pet lovers to keep an electronic dog or cat at home without the bother of having to feed, walk, or clean up after it. Likewise an electronic wood fire with no wood to stack and no ash to dispose of. I heard recently that the latest thing in zoos is to install television cameras in the wild and invite visitors to observe the animals on television screens in rooms in a central building. Having children see themselves on television at birthday parties is a more effective trick than producing a live magician; visiting by means of a videotape is a more effective boost to the morale of hospital patients than coming to the bedside in person.

Then there are the portable video cameras making their appearance in increasing numbers at tourist sites. Last year, while visiting the Tetons, my wife and I found ourselves standing next to a man who had a video camera on his shoulder and was conducting a strange monologue, as if he were addressing a hidden audience—which, of course, he was. He was recording his impression in sound and vision for what he imagined a television experience should be for an audience hidden in the future. To update Susan Sontag's famous observation, it was a sobering reminder of how reality today is experienced in terms of video images.[11]

Can there, indeed, be any serious doubt that television has worked a revolution in cultural habits as profound as the revolution worked by print in the second half of the fifteenth century? Whether illiteracy increases or remains normative for large numbers of viewers may not be relevant, for television has radically altered the habits of mind even of the reading public. Furthermore, the sheer volume of video material being produced by the VCR market itself poses a commercial threat to consumer spending on traditional reading matter, and more than one-half of the television population are already owners of home VCR sets. Those of us who still believe in the desirability of literacy will be bewildered, to say the least, by this new culture. I have had students who describe people who don't own a television set as deviants, fit for the madhouse; and of course it is true that if you don't view on a regular basis, you are a cultural oddity, not properly in tune with the times. You are deprived, or backward, in a new kind of way, as were illiterates in print culture. In fact, you are a new type of underclass, a lettered one, "an endangered species" in Kozol's term.[12]

Television, on the other hand, has at least given Americans something the United States lost at the Revolution in the sense of a mother

tongue containing the cultural and historical associations that define national consciousness. By providing a sense of common identity to the diverse groups that make up this pluralistic society, television has replaced
the need for such a mother tongue. The consequences of this shift in
the role of language in a television age must be profound for all mother
tongues, but none more so than English. The Peacock Report on the
BBC used an apt phrase to describe this attribute of television, perhaps
not giving it the weight that I do, and somewhat smugly, I think, claim-
ing it exclusively for the BBC. The report quotes a study that states that
"British broadcasting in its existing public service mode should and did
assert and reflect Britain as a community, society, and culture and that
it was the principal forum by which the nation as a whole was able to
talk to itself."[13]

*The principal forum by which the nation as a whole is able to talk to
itself*—does not this sum up the mirror-like nature of television's effect on
human consciousness? Most Americans want to view what everyone else
is viewing in order to confirm their sense of belonging. When, after the
Challenger disaster, President Reagan spoke of the nation keeping a vigil
by their television sets, he was testifying more truly than perhaps he realized to the new order of consciousness possessed by Late-Twentieth-
Century North American Persons: To view is to be. Selfhood is realized
in the knowledge that we are all watching the same image at the same
time.

From this shared reality, mediated by television, the myths of a
new age are born, nursery and household tales brought up to date. One
such myth is the apotheosis of President Kennedy following his assassi-
nation in November 1963, which happened to be the first time that television dominated media coverage of such an event. Here is no less a figure than Theodore White, himself a master of literary exposition,
testifying to television's role in creating this myth. White was in
Washington at the time, a guest in Averell Harriman's house. He writes:

> I would slip out of the house to pick for fragments of the story, and
> then dart back in to sit and watch on television to find out what was
> really happening. . . . Sitting with friends in Harriman's parlor and
> watching the tube was to be in touch with reality, to be part of the na-
> tional grief. But to slip out, to do one's reportorial duty, to ask ques-
> tions that must be asked, was a chore, for television tugged one back,
> irresistibly, to emotional participation.[14]

There are still benighted folk, some of them, I regret to say, colleagues, who say that television is nothing more than a delivery system for modes of address belonging to the old culture. This ostrich-like attitude ignores McLuhan's central insight into the communication process, that a medium's particular technology is all the time transmitting a psychological message to us, and it is this psychological message that alters our perception of reality. I must confess that much criticism of the present state of our culture strikes me as unreal (one might even say, "academic") as it is framed in terms that belong to a culture that is already passing away. Nothing is easier, as I am the first to admit, than to accuse television of being no more than "mindless entertainment," a favorite term of abuse among the intelligentsia. Even if every television program were to satisfy the tastes of an educated minority (a ghastly thought), the forms the medium employs to broadcast such programs would be the same and the psychological effect of these forms on viewers would be no less potent in transforming consciousness. To preserve the old cultural terms of reference means abandoning television altogether, a most desirable operation, according to my dear friend Malcolm Muggeridge, which he terms "having one's aerials removed" (in the age of cable, one might substitute "one's umbilical cord"). Jerry Mander's 1978 book, *Four Arguments For The Elimination of Television*, takes a similar view.

More to the point, I believe, are those who accept that television is here to stay and will remain the primary educational force in society, and who therefore call for restraint and greater social responsibility from media practitioners, an argument strongly made by John Silber in his recent book, *Straight Shooting*. Of course the viewing public also has to exercise restraint and self-discipline. Let us, however, remember that the affective quality of television lies in its technology. Its forms are educating as much as its content. It is the act of viewing that attracts viewers rather than specific programs.[15] Take "Sesame Street." In my opinion it is wishful thinking to suppose that "Sesame Street" is transmitting a message about reading books, or reading at all for that matter. But how powerful a tool "Sesame Street" is in teaching children to view television regularly, with great expectations, and to accept the authority of television over every other experience and authority in life, including the authority of parents and teachers!

Acknowledging, then, that television has swept over western culture with astonishing speed and radical impact to become the medium of all media, what can we say of its technological message, the message, that is specific to the medium? Television is a medium whose very nature repudiates the path of intellectual knowledge. In the presentation of information, factual or fictional, its essential form is drama—dramatic music, dramatic graphics, dramatic titles, dramatic delivery by announcers, dramatic cutting from one scene to another, one shot to another, and, though certainly not least, dramatic advertising pitches. Given the choice between two visual images, we will always take the stronger, the more dramatic one. What is being transmitted through this form, therefore, is predominantly emotional information. Eliminate these dramatic devices and you have no program. In fact, you don't have what we mean by "television." Nothing is more boring than a camera that never changes its angle or shot, nothing less likely to attract an audience, and so less capable of sending messages. Do you ever see a crowd around the monitors of security cameras? Without dramatic changes, we have entropy. If knowledge is measured by facts, names, dates, grasp of geography, of logical argument and the rational assessment of issues, then exposure to network news on television has no bearing on the acquisition of this kind of knowledge.[16]

If the information that television transmits is predominantly emotional, the mechanism by which this information is transferred lies in a complex system of audiovisual codes. And of all the technical forms of television, the cut, I believe, is the most fundamental, the one that most determines the hidden message of the medium, as type does with print.

Unlike the editing of feature films, where the cut follows the demands of linear storytelling (I'm speaking of film in its popular form), cutting from one television image to the next grew from the necessity in the early days of television to provide more than one picture of what was going on in the studio, be it a play, a panel discussion, an informational presentation, or a children's game. Originally these studio productions were live, which gave television its special drawing power, despite poor quality pictures. The illusion of being present at a live happening is what I believe still makes television appealing to large masses of people for large amounts of time and accounts for the high sales value of its supposed "reality." Viewers are able to share in the studio event in real time but in a manner unlike real life. The different viewpoints provided by cutting from one camera to the next, from one angle to another, are not freely chosen by viewers, as we might allow our eyes to stray across a hall or church gathering or theater stage in an experience directly affected by other members of the audience or congregation, as well as by the total

scene in front of us. In viewing a television program, the changing viewpoints are determined for us by the studio director according to a
logic—a language, if you will—peculiar to television itself.

Each time a cut is made a message is sent to the viewer saying,
"Look for meaning in this cut." On television, the cut is more potent in
its ability to attract attention than the action taking place between cuts.
It is what sets television apart from film, although many of the conventions of film are still apparent in television. Try turning the sound down
and note what catches your eye; it is the cut linking image to image
rather than action within each image. Yet it is the sound as often as not
that provides the excuse for the cut, a complex relationship between the
two senses. This relationship will often supply the organizational force
holding together a composite image made up of different shots, as in a
news story. When the eye and the ear are competing against each other,
usually the eye will win. But we need the ear to help us interpret the
image, even if this is only music, which always sends a strong emotional
signal. Television, indeed, is heavily dependent on its verbal elements,
the talking head being its commonest form, whether in factual or fictional shows or, at its most debased, in the sound bite of news. We
should note that in this hidden language, what must be avoided at all
costs is visual boredom. The intellectual content of words spoken is of
no importance; all that matters is the sound made by the words. Unlike
human speech in print-culture, where words are carriers of thought and
the expression in sound of human reason, speech in television-culture
plays the same role as a piano accompaniment in the days of silent
movies. It is a redundant tool to inform us of mood and to assist us in
reading the pictures, often aided, of course, by other sound effects, such
as laughter and applause. It is enough for us to understand the fury in
the words without our seeking, like Desdemona, to understand the
words themselves.

With cutting from image to image providing one form of condi-
tioning agent in the language of television, another comes from our habituation to the small size, rectangular shape, and poor quality of the visual frame itself. Tidily enclosed by the box of the television receiver, the
television frame is a frame within a frame. It presents us with a world
under our control, a world domesticated by our actual homey surroundings. In these surroundings we are not called on to suspend disbelief as
we don't disbelieve our own home, our furnishings, and family snap-
shots. On the contrary, we willingly commit ourselves to a belief in the

reality of the images. The more the images can be made to appear as real reality, the more we believe them, especially when it comes to "harm-inflicting actions."[17]

In itself, a television image is dull. It is so lacking in arousal that we need exaggerated sound and devices like the cut to maintain interest. Where the film frame utilizes every part of the screen for movement and effect, and with great beauty of color and composition, the small size and poor quality, at least until recently, of the television frame force us to present our representation of reality center screen. All that happens must happen before our eyes, and the images must hold "instant meaning" for most if not all of the viewing audience, so we rely on symbols and stereotypes to provide this instant meaning, like the codewords of speech. There is neither time nor readiness to explain what is unusual or difficult.[18] It follows, I think, that for most of the population what cannot be shown on television by a comparatively small repertoire of symbolic images does not exist. Reality is picture: without pictures, no reality. The result is a television world of grotesque disproportion, which presents, for instance, a major political problem when it comes to dealing with the images—or, more to the point, the lack of them—coming from closed societies like the Soviet Union. An example of this was the series of eight videotapes on Andrei Sakharov and his wife, Elena Bonner, produced by the KGB with hidden cameras from August 1984 to June 1986 and widely disseminated in the West.[19]

A further aspect of the television frame needs mentioning. The present ratio of the frame, four parts horizontal to three parts vertical, cruelly restricts what we can show of the outside world. The big landscape, the tall building, the vast expanses of ocean, sky, or space cannot be adequately represented on television. The ratio of the frame makes it impossible even to present a person standing upright with full effect. Too much unnecessary visual information is coming at us from the space on either side of that person—visual noise. It is the same with trees and the steeples of churches. The television frame forces us to look at the world as flat, horizontal, with no horizons. It does not invite us to raise our eyes to the heavens. Do these mechanical factors leave a psychological imprint?

To compensate for the limitations of the television frame, we must concentrate on detail, on close-ups, on a mosaic-like montage of images, and a dazzling array of visual tricks. In thus reducing the cosmos to the dimensions of a television screen, however, we introduce a new visual scale where small objects become unusually large and large objects small. Surely over time and with heavy viewing our visual perception of the natural world must change. Is it not the case that the world of ideas already suffers from a similar distortion?

Emotional arousal is what visual images are best at achieving. They are much better suited to this function than to making rational state-ments or even, according to Gombrich, to expressing feelings.[20] If drama is the essence of each image and each sound effect that make up a visual message, each television program is structured on the funda-mental dramatic principle of conflict, complication, resolution, or as I like to simplify it, the problem-solution formula. In fictional programs—serial dramas, Masterpiece Theater, sitcoms, and soaps—the employment of this dramatic principle is logical. Such is the weight of these programs in the daily schedule, however, that the formula has come to dominate all other programs, including those which are suppos-edly nonfictional. Here is a senior news executive instructing his staff: "Every news story should, without any sacrifice of probity or responsibil-ity, display the attributes of fiction, of drama. It should have structure and conflict, problem and denouement, rising action and falling action, a beginning, a middle and an end. There are not only the essentials of drama; they are the essentials of narrative."[21]

So how does it work? A typical news story would run like this: There's trouble again in the Middle East (conflict); the Arabs say one thing, the Israelis another, and the Soviets are trying to make things worse (complication); the president of the United States sends a special envoy to sort it out (resolution). The principle works just as effectively in television advertising. You're going out on a date, but (problem) you have B.O.! Solution: our soap!

In one form or another, the problem-solution formula underlies virtually every television message, and this fact, to my way of thinking, must build up in audiences a deep-seated expectation that all problems have solutions. Is not this expectation, so characteristic of the American psyche, present in the way we deal with religious as well as political af-fairs, moral and intellectual issues? If there are problems that have plagued mankind since the Garden of Eden, the solution is to change the ground rules.

I'd like to illustrate the necessity of studying the technical forms of television by describing a small visual event I happened to catch as it was being transmitted live in the summer of 1985. I say small, but as a leaf thrown on the surface of a river will show the direction of the current, so these small television events tell us of the strength of the hidden force beneath. The event took place in a courtroom in Rhode Island as the second trial of Claus von Bulow reached its climax. Had von Bulow attempted to murder his wife by injecting her with insulin? The jury sent word that they had agreed on their verdict, and a delay of fifteen minutes ensued so that the media could be ready, along with other participants such as von Bulow's current mistress, who until now had hidden herself in the control van of Cable News Network.[22] There was one camera in court, supplied by a Providence station and providing continuous coverage on a pool basis for the networks.

Here was live television with a scene of dramatic actuality ideally suited to the medium. Now I must interject a personal comment. When I joined the television service of the BBC, straight from university at a time when television was virtually unknown at home and at school, I joined a group of men and women whose education, like mine, had been in the classical tradition of the western Enlightenment. Products of a literate culture, we thought in terms of a literate audience. We were taught, and we believed, that you showed the audience the source of the information you were transmitting. If you were quoting from a document you showed the document, if there was a speech you recorded the speech, or the portion of it you wanted. Afterwards, perhaps, or on the side, you might take shots of the audience or other relevant material. That's how literate people, print people, people of the Enlightenment, think.

To return to the courtroom in Rhode Island. You are in control of the one camera in court. As the foreman of the jury stands up to announce the verdict in this highly publicized trial, a verdict eagerly awaited and much speculated upon, where do you point your camera?

I put this question regularly to my students, all typical Late-Twentieth-Century North American Persons, children of the television revolution. With rarely an exception, the class says: you point your camera at von Bulow. Why? Because we want to see his reaction as the verdict is given. In terms of their own transformed consciousness, the students are undoubtedly correct. Today's television audience does not want to see the source of factual information, because the medium is not transmitting this kind of information at all. It is transmitting emotional information. News is theater, a spectator sport, and what we want is drama. Here's NBC's Reuven Frank again: "The highest power of television journalism is not in the transmission of information but in the transmission of experience . . . joy, sorrow, shock, fear, these are the stuff of news."[23]

The three main networks all carried the von Bulow story, ABC and CBS making it their lead item. Their three audiovisual packages were virtually identical, for ABC and CBS, an average of five seconds per shot, for NBC, four seconds.

Analyzing the stories shot by shot, with their sound elements, we can see that what we have in each case is a composite image which says in sum "a trial," "a verdict." These are no more the direct reporting of a live event than Seurat's paintings are direct accounts of life on the banks of the Seine. Instead we have a tableau as in Madame Tussaud's wax-works museum, or better, a television equivalent of a musical: "Monday in the Court with Claus." What television news gives us is a representa-tion by means of types. The shots are chosen for their symbolic value, a value that derives more from fictional portrayals in the real soap operas and drama series to be seen every day and every night on network tele-vision than from the few cases of actuality like von Bulow's, which merit the attention of network news. Not for nothing did the news media call the von Bulow trial a soap opera. They would not have reported it had it been anything else.

Jurists I have spoken to express concern that by allowing television into the courtrooms, the real-life actors in these real dramas are turning out performances to match those of their fictional counterparts. A recent report on New York City's police pointed to the same concern. According to this report, the public's perception of police behavior was based on its fictional representation in television serial dramas, behavior the real life police found unreal and unprofessional. Nevertheless, some real-life police begin to ask themselves if they ought not to adapt their be-havior to that of their fictional counterparts in order to retain the good will of the public.[24] Study after study, like those conducted by the Media Institute in Washington, D.C., reveal a contrast between reality as por-trayed on television and reality as described by statistics and sociology.[25] But which reality is psychologically convincing?

Theodore White wrote of emotional participation. I have sug-gested that it is in television's forms that we should look for the medium's affective power, notably in the power of visual images medi-ated by editing techniques in which music and sound play important parts. I do not say that the manifest program content is of no importance, but its interest lies mainly in showing us how age-old themes are being adapted to the new medium's technology.

If television is creating its own symbolic world, what has happened to the symbols and rituals of the pre-television age, particularly those used in religious ceremonies? The question, of course, is central to our discussion of today's values and icons. Can the traditional Christian liturgies, for example, be transferred successfully to the television screen? How is the Word to be expressed in a television age?

Many of us have been troubled by these questions for a long time. We find it hard to reconcile ourselves to the reality of television and are tempted to take a negative position. Muggeridge likens television to a twentieth-century golden calf.[26] But we can't, of course, tell how things will work out in a hundred years from now, and we must remember that each new mode of communication contains its predecessors within it. I can imagine scribes meeting with mulled wine in their refectories in the early sixteenth century and complaining that style was being destroyed by this new uniform type, and the authority of the church was being undermined in matters of education and morals by these upstart, self-promoting printers, and all for commercial gain. Are there not various churches today, not ecclesiastical ones, who take the same line?

To return to the thesis advanced by Walter Ong, that a radical change in the technology of communication leads to a radical change in human consciousness, I venture to suggest that, paradoxical as it may seem, one consequence of prolonged exposure to the technology of television is to increase the tension between what we see and what we believe. Is what we see orderly or anarchic? There are those who argue that regular viewers of television are left with a greatly strengthened sense of chaos since the general impression given by such prolonged viewing is of an unstable world where disasters, natural and manmade, are the norm, where verbal and physical strife is seen to be uppermost in all public and private conduct, and where moral confusion reigns in the affairs of government, corporations, and private life. Television, in this view, is a blend of nihilism and hedonism. The people sit down to eat and drink and rise up to play. This television world is a world "without much coherence or sense" in Neil Postman's eyes, the eyes of one devoted to literacy and rationalism.[27]

Against this pessimistic diagnosis we must weigh the force of the medium's own codes and conventions and remind ourselves of what Gombrich calls "the beholder's share," namely, what viewers bring to their viewing. With the mass audience, which is most of the population, including the educated elite, certain expectations are inculcated as to the amount of the givens in life. One of these expectations is the program schedule itself, which exercises an iron discipline over the networks because of the demands of affiliates and advertisers and competitive planning. However much some viewers say they object to commercial breaks, we know that they will come at points of rising tension, that each commercial will run for a set term, now usually thirty seconds, and that programs will change on the hour or the half hour. Such scheduling procedures are part of the rhythm of television life. To break them, as when we go live for an unrehearsed event, is a deeply unsettling experience.

Also belonging to the regular beat of television life is the dramatic structure I've mentioned, the problem-solution formula, as well as the standardization of production techniques linking visual image, musical feeling, and verbal comment. Though television has had a radical impact on culture, it has, I think, proved to be a conservative force in holding society together, at least in democracies. In other parts of the world, as a symbol of modernity, television may perhaps encourage change and the displacement of sacred cows. Is it too much to suggest that the message of the cut in television, a cut that joins as well as severs, signaling a beginning as well as an end, is to accustom us to change within order? And though the information being transmitted with each message is emotional, are we not convinced that beneath the sending of each message there is a rational force at work? Furthermore, does not television's technology make it possible to look forward to a new kind of language, one that transcends mother tongues and national barriers, one that may persuade the human race that it has a common destiny?

These considerations lead me to think that the television revolution may, after all, amount to a massive reinforcement of mankind's intuitive sense that there is order and meaning in the universe, a reinforcement, therefore, of the religious instinct. And by the same token, this sense must also lead to a massive rejection of atheistic materialism and philosophies based on chance.

Where, then, does the word migrate to in the world of television? God, of course, alone knows for sure. The word on television is not an event in time nor an object in space, for television has abolished time and space, nor is the word on television solely an image, though it may be revealed in images. The word on television is perhaps more like a happening, an experience of the heart. For myself, though mystified, I do not believe this excludes the possibility, any more than earlier media revolutions did, of individuals coming to know the word made flesh.

– 3 –

Television and the Shaping of Cognitive Skills

Renee Hobbs

Everyone knows that television has tremendous influence even though the word "influence" has been bandied about so much that it almost seems trivial. Nevertheless, for 30 or 40 years we've been hard-pressed to describe the nature of that influence. What is well documented is the way that people's behavior and attitudes are affected by the content of what they see on television. We have documentation on violence on television and its influence on behavior; on television's portrayal of sexuality; on consumer socialization; and how the content of advertising messages has influence.[1] However, if we think that only the content of television programming influences our society, we greatly underestimate the potency of the medium.

What I want to discuss are some of the social consequences resulting from the very form and structure of the medium; more specifically, I want to address the impact of format and editing conventions of television. My hypothesis is that two aspects of the structure of the medium, television format and television editing conventions, are both extremely powerful vehicles that reflect and shape the cognitive processes of attention, organization, interpretation, and prediction. Thus, in effect, I am proposing a mechanism for understanding *how* television influences culture and values, because although the content of television influences culture and values, so does its form, in highly specific and predictable ways.

We know that communication media, like language and television, are not simply vehicles for transmitting messages, not simply pipes through which we send messages. If they were, they wouldn't be so powerful. Communication media serve not only as vehicles for transmitting messages; they are used in creating and developing messages—that is, they are used in thought. We have internalized communications media, just as we have internalized language, so that these media can be used not only to transmit messages but as tools to think with.[2]

Early filmmakers surely exploited the new medium in ways that illustrate the relationship between media and mental processes. Consider the creative power of early filmmakers as they used celluloid to construct messages. Techniques like the close-up and the zoom are symbolic codes that are analogues of everyday patterns of visual attention. In some sense the zoom represents the actions we engage in when we pay attention, because when we pay attention, we move to focus on a single small part of the scene, and everything else blurs and disappears in the background. Filmmakers, either consciously or unconsciously, invented techniques of manipulating the distance between the camera and the subject which externalize this process of perception. Close-ups, long shots, and zooms are representations of a very complex mental skill—paying attention. A number of the editing conventions of television may be perceptual analogues of mental processes, which may explain why it is so easy to watch television. In fact, my colleagues and I developed the following experiment to get at this very issue.

The experiment was designed to test some assumptions regarding media literacy. For about 15 years now, we have been bombarded with the concept of media literacy. This concept is informed by the notion that the symbol systems of television, the editing conventions, are similar to print, in that viewers must learn how to decode them.[3] But do viewers need practice and experience with the medium to be able to decode editing conventions? Scholars have considerable evidence on how children understand television and know that some combination of age and experience is necessary to process television images accurately.[4] And of course, very young children don't decode television so well as adults.[5] With all the research evidence, however, it is unclear whether developmental factors regarding age or experience with the medium are essential prerequisites for understanding the editing conventions.

The question is, how do you find a population that has had no experience with television? Certainly none exists in this country! But in some remote areas of the world, there are some groups of people who have never seen films or television, although each year this population diminishes. Such a population could be used to help investigate whether editing conventions are comprehensible to adult viewers with no familiarity with film or television. The Pokot people of western Kenya are such a people. They have never seen television, never seen film, never seen two-dimensional representations like photographs or maps. They live in an environment virtually as close to a tribal culture as exists in the twentieth century, the perfect group for a naturalistic experiment. We showed them two versions of a television program that we made using plausible occurrence in the village.[6] In one version, we turned the camera on, let the narrative event proceed in front of the camera as if it were a proscenium stage. When the narrative event was over, we turned the camera off.

In the second version, we used only one editing convention: manipulated point-of-view. In other words, we changed the relationship between the camera and the subject using close-ups, medium shots, and long shots. In a three-minute narrative event, we used 13 edit points or "cuts." The content of both versions was otherwise identical. The length of the broadcast was identical. The only difference between these two broadcasts was that one had no editing at all, and the other had 13 edit points manipulating point-of-view, the distance between the camera and the subject.

What we found was rather surprising. We found that there were no differences in the ability of the tribal villagers to comprehend the message. The villagers who saw the edited version were just as competent at decoding as were the villagers who saw the unedited version. With no experience with the medium, these villagers were perfectly adept at decoding this mediaspecific symbol system, namely, point-of-view narration. Based on our research, we believe that some editing conventions are perceptual isomorphs of experience: You don't need experience with the medium to learn to decode them. This explains why television is so easy to watch, why it takes so little effort for us to decode, why it takes no mental effort to watch television. From this it follows that the representational codes of film and television can also help to develop or degenerate the cognitive skills of attention, comprehension, interpretation, and prediction.

Television and Attention

The relationship between television and attention is the area in which we have the best evidence for understanding television's influence. Writing in the early years of the twentieth century, Hugo Munsterberg was the first experimental psychologist recruited by William James at Harvard to begin the experimental laboratory. He was also an aficionado of film, which in the beginning of the twentieth century was exploding with creative new techniques and devices for manipulating the expressive potential of the medium. Munsterberg made some remarkable observations about the similarities he saw between editing conventions and attention. He viewed the close-up as an externalization of the process of paying attention, and in the same way, viewed the flashback as a technique for representing memory just as the flash-forward externalized the mental skills of imagining.[7]

It is absolutely remarkable to read a psychologist more than 70 years ago making these observations and, although the argument seems somewhat simplified in retrospect, it represents the first time psychologists looked at the relationship between the products that we use in creating film and video and the processes that we use inside our head.

We have more empirical evidence on the relationship between children's attention and editing conventions than about most other topics in the field of media studies. Researchers know that young children between the ages of two and five seem compelled to attend to editing conventions, and certain editing conventions draw the attention of children more than others.[8] Those editing conventions are ones that include high movement, rapid pacing, lots of edit points, and loud music. These editing conventions are intense in the use of movement that is perceptually salient, which compels attention. Researchers have discovered that young children are compelled to watch the screen when those editing conventions are used, but that over time, children are able to control their attentional behavior; that is, older children are not so compelled to watch the screen when those editing conventions are used. This bears a close relationship to what we know about the human perceptual system. Our eyes are designed to actively monitor change. It is built-in, hard-wired, as it were, into the perceptual system.[9] Younger children don't have very much control over using that perceptual system, and so they are compelled to watch the intense movement on the screen. And those of us who have seen children that age watching television can see the intensity with which their attention is drawn to the screen. Older children are better able to mediate their attentional skills and control that behavior.

Although over time we gain control, even adults find this array of movement and visual changes on the TV screen compelling. Think of the time when you were in a conversation and the television was on in the room. Sometimes, no matter how interesting the conversation might happen to be, no matter how much you wanted to participate in the conversation, you found your eyes being drawn inexplicably to the screen. It is an attentional behavior that even adults find difficult to control. In this way, then, editing conventions shape attention patterns by capitalizing on our natural instinct to monitor changes in the visual display.

Television formats also interact with our attentional skills in a way that serves a useful function. After all, we watch television at home, in an environment with multiple distractions and multiple possible activities. Thus the predictability of certain kinds of formats, like the sitcom, the game show, the drama, even the commercial, permit us to allocate our attention very selectively. For example, young people will often walk out of the room when a program is on that they are supposed to be watching. If you ask them about it, they are very candid: "I don't have to watch now; I don't have to watch until after the commercial." Viewers engage in multiple activities while watching television because we have learned how to allocate our attention by our familiarity with program formats. The format of the medium simplifies the processes of paying attention, making it possible to watch television in conjunction with other activities of daily life.

Although generations of teachers and parents and physicians and psychologists have talked about the degeneration of our attention span owing to the influence of television, we have very little empirical evidence to support that belief. When you talk to teachers, especially older elementary school teachers who have been teaching in the schools for years, and who can compare the children of the 1950s and 1960s with the children of the 1970s and the 1980s, they will frequently comment on the decreased attention span of children and attribute these differences to the influence of television.

According to many media scholars, television presents a fragmented set of images and sounds, and that fragmentation becomes paralleled in our own attentional skills.[10] Because we are used to receiving fragmented information and information in discontinuous form, we come to prefer that form; and information, such as a formal lecture, that requires sustained attention over a long period of time, becomes more difficult because it is not habitually required in our culture. Consequently, it takes a great deal of effort and discipline to make the attentional adjustment to a formal lecture of 60 minutes or more, for it is an adjustment that runs against the grain of discontinuity.

Television and the Skills of Organization and Interpretation

Researchers can easily tell whether someone is paying attention or not. However, it is not so easy to examine the "black box" of the rest of the cognitive process. How are you encoding this information in memory? What meaning are you making of it? We have relatively little understanding of the way in which television affects the skills of organization and interpretation, primarily because those skills must be inferred. They are invisible to us except through indirect examination.

Nevertheless, I want to say more about how television affects how we store, organize, and interpret information by discussing television news. Researchers who examine viewers' ability to comprehend television almost always use television news programming because, given the manner in which the news is presented, it is easier to measure this mode of learning directly. The broadcast news on the major networks present us with isolated snippets of information: 45 seconds on upcoming elections, 100 seconds on business and economics, 35 seconds on health and science. Those snippets make it easy for viewers by permitting us to decide whether or not to encode that information. Clearly, the conventions and formats of television help us encode information from a television program in ways which are most profitable to the commercial medium.

For example, my understanding of economics is at such a rudimentary level that I don't bother to encode televised economic news in my memory, even though I may pay attention to it. Because my understanding of economics is not well developed enough for me to encode the information into my existing set of knowledge and beliefs, it simply slips by; and because this information is only on for a few seconds, it slips by easily. On the other hand, for science and health stories, politics or sports, I have a well-developed array of information. Thus, when I hear the cue for science and health or sports, I pay more attention and I actively encode this information into my existing knowledge.

In a sense then, isolated snippets are valuable: they help viewers retrieve information about which they already have well-developed schemas for understanding. On the other hand, television's isolated snippets do not help viewers encode information in memory if they don't have sufficient prior knowledge. The 45 seconds on economics or the 35 seconds on elections make it impossible to encode that information if viewers don't have an understanding of that topic to begin with.[11] In other words, a few seconds of information is not going to help develop the schemata viewers need to encode this information. Therefore, television's isolated news snippets do help to acquire information rapidly about topics already known. But conversely, the isolated snippets inhibit the ability to encode information on topics that viewers don't know very much about. Watching television news, then, really only helps viewers to reinforce what they already know; it does very little to make them more sophisticated in these topics other than to provide a few new bits of data.

Doris Graber comments on the obvious value implication of such behavior:

> When people fail to learn or create appropriate schemas for certain types of news, that news cannot be absorbed. The socialization of average Americans apparently leaves a number of gaps in schema structure. These gaps then make it difficult to focus public attention on some important problems. News about most foreign countries or news about science are examples. Even when such news is presented in simple ways, most of the audience fails to make the effort to absorb it because appropriate schemas did not form part of past socialization.[12]

Thus the simplicity of television news makes it possible for only a few viewers to extract meaningful information and excludes others who simply don't have a well-developed understanding of those current events. "What will happen," Graber asks, "to the quality of learning about public affairs if newspaper use continues to decline and electronic media capture an increasing share of the audience's attention?"

The answer seems obvious enough. Owing to the limitations imposed by the commercial format, television network news is unable to

provide us with sufficient background and information to help us develop schemas for understanding complex events in places like the
Middle East and Central America. Therefore, unless you already know
something about these topics, unless you know, at the very least, where
the Middle East and Central America are (and we've recently discovered
that upwards of 50% of Americans do not know such elementary geographic facts) television news will be of no assistance in helping you develop your understanding in these areas.

The economic and commercial constraints on television as a
medium of information are critical here, for television's failure to inform
and to edify is not due to a limitation inherent in the medium itself. It
is not inherent in the medium of television that a "cut" has to be made
every three seconds, that the pacing and rhythm have to be what it
presently is, causing viewers to change channels every 3.7 minutes.[13] In
fact, the present shape, look, and feel of television are not due to the inherent capabilities of the medium, but are a result of the economic environment in which the medium was initially created and in which it, for
the most part, continues. In other words, when we look at the format of
television and when we think of the interpretive framework that television provides, we cannot overlook the economic forces that created these
formats.

In the 1950s during the so-called "Golden Age of Television,"
there was a lot of experimentation and a diversity of social views were
presented. "CBS Playhouse 90," Paddy Chayefsky's "Marty," and many
other programs presented complex views of American social life. But
such ambitious, socially relevant, and intellectually challenging programming has become obsolete, because of the influence of advertisers who
looked for programs that provided a pleasant atmosphere in which to
portray their product.[14] Do you want your soap advertisement shown
next to a difficult and complex portrayal of social crises in America, or
programming that generates ambiguity regarding the relationship between power and the disenfranchised? Or do you want your product put
in an environment that shows American middle-class people at their
best, with healthy, white, smiling faces and beautiful teeth?

Decisions to minimize this kind of ambiguity were systematically
made in the fifties and they have persisted to this day. In the 1980s programs emphasize affluence. Of course, "Dallas" and "Dynasty" are the
first examples that come to mind. But think of programs that appear to
us rather innocuous, like "The Cosby Show." The affluence which

underlies this program is almost invisible. We don't even pay attention to it, yet it is part of the very fabric of the messages, the messages that represent the format, that represent the way advertisers and broadcasters want us to see ourselves and our society. In this sense, consider the broadcasting strategy called LOP ("least objectionable programming"), developed in the early 1960s. By the very economic nature of television, which has to appeal to the most number of viewers to be successful, the least objectionable programming strategy appeals to the largest number of viewers. Such a strategy has a very definite influence on the format of television, which in turn has a direct influence on messages communicated through television. By permitting this medium to evolve as it has, we have as a consequence reduced the diversity of media formats and messages, so that television formats reinforce mainstream social views.

Even with the increasing number of channels available with cable television, there is little diversity because it is still restricted by the prevailing formats. Michael Schudson comments: "These conventions help make culturally consonant messages readable and culturally dissonant messages unsayable. Their function is less to increase or decrease the truth value of the messages they convey than to shape or narrow the range of what kind of truths can be told."[15] Television formats reinforce certain assumptions about the political world, the social world, and the world of values as well.

Television and the Skills of Prediction and Expectation

When we pay attention, organize, encode, and interpret information, we are led to pay attention again and to make new choices. That is the cognitive skill of prediction and expectation, and in many ways it is television that has shaped our expectations about all elements of our culture, from politics to religion. And here I argue that repeated exposure to television format and editing conventions sets viewer expectations, directly shaping cultural and social values.

For example, I have found, over the years of teaching, that I have a difficult time trying to introduce video art to college students. My students sit patiently through video art pieces and after it is all over, say, "Huh? What is it? It's not a sitcom, it's not a game show, it's not a news program, it's not a documentary. What is it?" It's not good, because it doesn't fit their expectations about what television is. Now this is a very

difficult objection to counteract, because they are telling me very explicitly that the conventions that exist on broadcast television are identical
with television itself. Such conventions are good because students and
the rest of us have been exposed to them over and over again. Many
video artists combat this strategy by satirically playing on these conventions, manipulating and altering them. But that is still playing within the
realm of our existing expectations.

Let us reflect on programs that do not use the editing conventions
of network television with its rapid pacing, slickness, and visual intensity. Is it inherent in the medium that to be successful you have to use
those conventions? Is it inherently bad television to portray, for example,
a talking head? Is there something, as Murray-Brown (Chapter 2, this
book) and Postman suggest, basically boring about that? I don't think
so. I think it has rather to do with our expectations, which develop over
time. I do not think it is inherent to the medium that we have to prefer
rapid pacing and ten-second sound bites to longer shots of people speaking in full sentences and paragraphs.

Viewers, however, through their repeated exposure to television,
demand those conventions. Thus, for example, PBS, in order to be successful and to compete for viewers, has been forced to present educational and instructional programming with those techniques intact,
using the conventions of commercial television to teach about culture,
values, science, and all the rest.[16] And consider the multiple reasons why
local access cable television programming failed to attract viewers, leading to its virtual demise. One reason is that people didn't watch it. Why
didn't people watch it? It didn't look like "good" television. Viewers
comment: "They only had two cameras; it was unprofessional; it didn't
look good." Note here that reference to content is irrelevant; reference is
rather to form and appearance. It didn't look like commercial television,
and so it didn't attract viewers. Why fund such an endeavor? Through
repeated exposure to a limited number of formats and a uniform pattern
of editing conventions, our expectations have already been set as to what
is good and what is bad on television. These expectations are not inherent to the medium, but are the result of repeated exposure to the conventions already familiar to us.

Obviously, the hegemony of commercial broadcasting formats has
an influence on viewers' ability to accept new formats. In this regard, we
have had an interesting naturalistic experiment in American television
during the 1980s: the advent of music television, the first example of a

dramatically new format in television in a long time. Music television, when it started in 1981, originally used a variety of formats, which are, however, hard to describe in words. Forget for a moment the arguments regarding the content of music television, the sexual and violent images and messages. The structure and the form of music television in 1981 was considerably more diverse then than it is now at the end of the decade. Only three or perhaps only two formats are commonly used on music television today: the narrative format, where a story is portrayed (like a little sitcom or soap compressed into three minutes), and the performance video (which has the musician displayed in all his or her splendor). Some would argue that the restriction of format in music television is probably a result of economic issues, so that record companies who are spending a lot of money don't take risks, and go with what's safe. While this argument has conventional feasibility, I would argue that the reduction in format is due rather to a sensitivity to what viewers like: a conventional format in music videos just as in everything else on television. Viewers like familiar formats. This is an empirical fact. They like narrative and performance videos, since narrative videos are easy to understand, are comfortable, and performance videos don't require much mental effort at all. Producers are responding to the interests of their audience; thus they deliberately reduce the diversity of formats.

Finally, it is clear that formats also influence our understanding and expectations regarding message content. As television becomes the dominant medium in our society, in our culture, we sense that it has influence far beyond itself and that it has a tremendous influence upon other media, especially print media. For example, the newspaper *USA TODAY* explicitly models its form on television; indeed, it is television-inspired. It is highly graphic, pictorial in nature, and brief and fragmented; one rarely has to jump to an inside page to finish reading anything in *USA TODAY*. Its fragmentation is its value because it doesn't take very long to read. You can't spend more than twenty minutes on *USA TODAY* even if you are among the slowest readers.

In other words, television format has determined public expectations regarding all formats, at least for the mass public, which itself influences the elite public more than we would like to admit. Television formats not only influence television but all other aspects of culture. It is precisely in this sense that formats and editing conventions have their greatest power.

Television's prominence in our society is neither good nor bad in terms of inherent value. But television's restrictions of formats and editing conventions can shape our expectations so that we are not exposed to a full range of information and ideas. Here is where the medium is potentially dangerous. It is here that specific value judgments intrude. By its ability to shape our interest in information, television editing conventions and formats encourage a value system that emphasizes fragmentation over continuity, repetition over diversity, and familiar messages over unfamiliar ones, all of it in 30-second bits instead of more sustained attentional patterns. It is this video legacy that has shaped modern American politics and business and religion and culture, not through the messages presented on television, but through specific utilizations of the form and structure of the medium itself.

– 4 –

The Emperor Has Only Clothes:
Toward a Hermeneutic of the Video Text

Lenore Langsdorf

Paul Goldberger, in the *New York Times*, distinguishes "those arts that are by nature visual, like architecture, from those that are not primarily visual, like music." He goes on to observe:

> But what is happening in both fields is not so dissimilar. In architecture, we see visual complexity put aside in favor of intense, easy visual impact. In music and theater, we see musical or verbal ideas nearly overwhelmed by a mode of expression that is supposed to serve them, not dominate them.
>
> Sometimes this happens . . . where there is so little inherent substance behind all the visual excess that we might easily say the emperor has no clothes—or more properly, that the emperor has only clothes. . . . [This] does little to expand the bounds of traditional theater, for it is not, in the end, of the theater. . . . Its ancestor, really, is television.[1]

The frequent absence of that "inherent substance" of ideas in contemporary cultural production is the topic of this chapter. On the basis of a consideration of the formal features of lived experience, verbal text, and video text, I propose that certain ideas, which are foundational for our sense of value, are intrinsically absent in the video text. In other words, I find that the video text, by virtue of its formal structure—and thus distinct from the programming which is that text's content—disinherits the sort of meaningfulness that is foundational for our traditional recognition and assessment of value.

This is not necessarily a disinheritance to be regretted. It may be a matter of clearing away transient or archaic ideas without which we are just as well off, perhaps even better off. It may also be the necessary correlative to developing different ideas, recognizing other forms of meaningfulness, and instituting alternative values. Thus, I would stress at the outset that I am analyzing certain formal features of video text, rather than condemning either the form or content, technology or programming, syntax or semantics, of television as such. It is on the basis of that analysis that I propose correlations between formal, syntactical features and certain ideas, and I also propose that these ideas give substance, and thus value, to a text. I do not, however, want to fold the evaluation of those ideas—as meaningful and valuable—into the description of their presence and absence. Clearly, Goldberger regrets the lack of substance in current cultural productions. But we need to consider whether this regret is simply a manifestation of his, and our, proclivity for our literary heritage. Goldberger is a verbal-textual person and, like all scholars, has a fondness for the written word. Without adopting value egalitarianism, then, I do want to look carefully at what we may be losing and what we may be gaining, before bemoaning or extolling the presence or absence of ideas in the video text.

One way to focus on this issue is by reflecting on just what is involved in our fondness for the written word. One ability comes to mind quite readily: We are generally able to appropriate meaning from a text. We can understand the ideas and trains of thought that authors develop; we can recognize and assess their arguments (in both a loose and a logical sense of the term); and we can assess the relative value of those ideas and arguments.[2]

Those who teach humanities courses at the university level, however, will probably agree that many, if not most, of our students do not share our verbal-text proclivity. Correlatively, they have difficulty in understanding the ideas presented in the texts used in these courses, in following arguments in these works, and in assessing the value of what is proposed by these authors. Since my experience seems to be fairly typical, I will cite it as a means of focusing on this difficulty. As a member of a small philosophy department in a large state university, I teach a large number of undergraduate students who are not philosophy majors. Most of those students are business or engineering majors who are in the Liberal Arts College because of certain required courses in English and History and a less precise stipulation that they take a few additional hours of humanities by choosing among electives in the college. In teaching such students who happen to take an introductory philosophy course in order to fulfill the humanities requirement, I have found a widespread, indeed, almost universal, inability to understand and evaluate the ideas presented in the traditional texts of our cultural and philosophical heritage.

Perhaps the clearest evidence of this inability is that when asked to identify, paraphrase, and evaluate an argument developed over an extended text (for example, Socrates' argument for granting him a pension in the *Apology*, or Luther's argument for free will in *Treatise on Christian Liberty*, or Descartes' argument for systematic doubt in *Discourse on Method*), students will usually merely rehearse the conclusion. When pushed on the question of *why* the author states that conclusion, the almost universal response is that it arises out of the author's "opinion" or "feeling." In other words, students typically do not distinguish between the text's *position* and the author's *opinion*. Thus any attempt to criticize a position is taken as criticism of the author. When criticism is directed toward a student's own work, that is, when the student is the author, defensiveness along the lines of "everyone's entitled to his or her own opinion, and this is mine" is the common rejoinder.

As I came to identify this problem in my introductory philosophy courses and discussed it with colleagues in other departments and institutions, I discovered that they have similar experiences. I found the same pattern in teaching "critical thinking" (in contrast to "philosophical classics") courses, this time in connection with sections in two different textbooks that dealt with the distinction between 'cause' and 'reason'. Clearly, this distinction was most difficult for students to comprehend. In discussing this problem with my colleagues I came to the tentative conclusion that students typically *explain* a conclusion as the effect of a psychological motivation that functions (more or less) like a physical cause. What is almost always absent is the ability, disposition, or skill that enables *understanding* the *conclusion* on the basis of the reasons provided for it, as distinct from *explaining* the *author* in cause-and-effect terms.[3] To put this distinction a little differently, students typically confuse the difference between providing psychological explanations for the author's *opinions*, and understanding the manner in which a given author has developed *reasons* for the argument that makes the text meaningful. The former approach has to do with what I term *explanatory reasoning*, and the latter requires what I call *interpretive reasoning*. Clearly, students typically have far more difficulty with the latter process. But why should this be the case?

A typical student majoring in business and who characterized himself as "good in math" provided a clue. He said that he was doing well in the classes for his major, but that he was "afraid" of his literature and philosophy classes. Both philosophy and literature, he said, involve a lot of "abstract reasoning" that is very different from the "concrete problems" involved in his business courses. Another clue came from a question, or more accurately, a complaint, by students frequently heard by my colleagues who teach literature: "Why do they take so long to get to the point, and use such fancy language to do it? Why don't they simply tell you what they mean?" Can it be that what seems so long-winded and abstract to many students is the form of organization in philosophical texts, a form quite different from the temporal (chronological) and spatial ordering that predominates in texts with a plot. For example, the plot of Socrates *Apology* can be summarized quite easily in a few brief sentences: Socrates was put on trial for corrupting the youth and being an atheist. He said that he was doing the state a favor by encouraging people to ask searching questions, and thus should be given a pension. But the court didn't appreciate the favor and sentenced him to death. What is left out of this simple summary of plot, of course, is all of the "abstract reasoning" about ideas and values that this dialogue provides. Yet this is precisely what teachers usually want students to understand and evaluate in humanities courses.[4] Typically, we consider both literary and philosophical texts worth studying in these courses to the extent that they are "substantial"; that is, they enable us to explore and assess the ideas they present.

It also occurred to me that while literary texts are organized by means of plot, they frequently use another mode of organization, which is the primary mode of philosophical texts. The narrative form usually relies on a spatial and chronological structure familiar to us all in our daily lives. To some degree, expository texts also rely on spatial and temporal organization, but more abstract, theoretical, conceptual, and philosophical texts rarely use any spatial or temporal structure. Rather, they provide a series of alternative ideas. In the course of discussion or out-right philosophical argument, the reader comes to see some of these ideas as being more important than others: as the conclusion of a line of reasoning, for example, or the point of a consideration that juxtaposes or unifies disparate themes so as to provide the basis for comparison, contrast, evaluation, and judgment. In other words, what occurs in *literary* and *philosophical* texts is the development of ideas that are evaluated as more or less important and valuable.

Because literary and philosophical texts demand that we recognize the relative value or importance of reasons for a conclusion, rather than follow the chain of events that form the plot structure of a narrative, they provide a clue as to why the sorts of ideas that give substance seem lacking in much contemporary cultural production. For it is true that following a plot requires that we recognize spatial and temporal organization or ordering, and reflection upon space and time certainly leads quickly to major philosophical questions. But we also have a commonsense understanding of spatial and temporal modes of organization that, in effect, allows us to bypass those questions in everyday situations. In other words, we use spatial and temporal forms of organization in our actual lived experience (our physical and social environments) as well as in our verbal experience, both oral and textual (conversation, reading, and writing). However, reflection upon the notion of value suggests that we lack a correlative commonsensical understanding that allows us to recognize and use that idea in an immediate, nonproblematic way. In other words, we do not seem to have at hand an understanding of what importance and value are. Nor do we have an immediate recognition of organization in terms of those ideas, correlative to our immediate, nonproblematic recognition of spatial and temporal organization.

In what follows, I explore this difference in forms of organization. I then connect the results of that exploration with the difficulties students have in understanding *substantial* texts, which explore ideas rather than recount events. I begin from an understanding of *value* as an idea that connotes positive importance and/or substance, and ask what connotations are involved in the recognition and use of the idea of value.

The Oxford English Dictionary is enlightening here, for it reveals that the terms "value," "valor," and "valid" all derive from the Latin *valere* ("to be strong"). Here we have a complex of meanings suggesting worth, import, esteem, authority, power, significance, and also "the quality of mind which enables a person to face danger with boldness or firmness; courage or bravery . . . ; well founded and fully applicable to the particular matter or circumstances; sound and to the point; against which no objections can fairly be brought."[5] These meanings have in common a resistance and even inaccessibility to visualization, at least, visualization in its ordinary sense. We can depict actions that may exemplify or suggest some of them. In contrast, we can depict, quite easily and even inevitably, the spatial arrangement of entities. We also have a variety of conventions for portraying temporal (chronological) arrangement. It seems, however, that value can be discussed and described, but cannot be directly portrayed or depicted.

I have written just now of four ways in which ideas can be presented to us: depiction, portrayal, description, and discussion. These terms signify a spectrum of accessibility to visualization and verbalization: All ideas, I would argue, are verbally accessible and communicable, although some can also be communicated and made accessible visually. The spectrum of accessibility I note here ranges from depiction, which aims simply to present an image by means of spatial correlation to the item depicted, to portrayal, which intends to convey something of the image's meaning. My passport picture, for instance, is supposed to present simply a visual image of me as the person entitled to use that document. A portrait, however, whether photographic or painted in oils, presents those features the artist chooses in order to portray my character, personality, or meaning as an individual person. I should note immediately that these extremes of the visual accessibility spectrum are ideal points specified for analytic purposes, rather than actualities. Selection is inherent in all perception. Thus, no depiction can simply transfer all and only the spatial features and organization of an image. On the other extreme, a portrayal must preserve something of its subject matter's spatial features and arrangement, if it is to succeed in conveying any idea of that subject matter.

At the verbal end of this spectrum, description correlates to depiction and discussion corresponds to portrayal. The difference between these verbal activities may be brought out by reflecting on the practice of a family counselor in talking with a troubled parent or spouse. The counselor is minimally interested in descriptions of the spouse or child on whom the trouble focuses. Although he or she may well begin an initial session by saying something like, "Describe your husband for me," we understand that a series of statistics giving spatial and temporal features—height, weight, age, color of eyes—is merely the beginning of the expected response. Thus, description and discussion are analytic rather than actual extremes. In other words, I introduce them as ideal types, rather than as categories of real examples.

We need one further set of distinctions before we can use these four ideal types (depiction, portrayal, description, and discussion) as the basis for an analysis aiming at understanding the presence and absence of value in different modes of cultural production. There may well be some ideas that are, in fact, most available visually, and others for which verbal access and communication is most effective. An example of the former would be fine distinctions in mood that can be conveyed by body language such as different smiles and postures. On the other hand, fine distinctions in quantity, and perhaps also in quality, are best communicated verbally. This variety is further enriched when we notice that there are four rather different ways in which our verbal and visual abilities are exercised. Two of these are natural or intrinsic to us as a species, but two others are technological; in other words, we have invented them rather than inherited them from our nature as human beings. Developmentally, the earliest mode of access to ideas is lived experience in which we combine vision with other forms of physical activity. We move our heads from side to side at birth and become increasingly mobile thereafter. Within two years we are adept at verbal communication. As we grow to adulthood, we combine these natural abilities with two technologically dependent abilities that radically change our natural lived experience of time and space. We elaborate upon what we see by inventing ways to produce two- and three-dimensional images: sketches, statues, mosaics, paintings, photographs, film, video; and we elaborate upon what we speak through the invention of writing, printing, and audio recording.[6]

Our inventiveness in regard to both seeing and speaking results in losses and gains. Our visual inventions allow us to see what is too far or too small to be seen naturally, as well as to see what cannot (except in a very limited way, by natural mirrors) be seen naturally, namely, seeing ourselves in a range of activities. These inventions are surely gains, but they come at the expense of sundering visual experience from the other forms of experience that naturally accompany it. We see more but at the cost of simplifying what is seen. Arguably, the gain is also a loss, although we are so accustomed to our unnatural, technologically elaborated lived experience that what is lost probably is not noticed until the experience is subjected to phenomenological analysis.

In order to do that sort of analysis, and then return to the issue of gain and loss in technologically elaborated experience, I shall now use one example in two ways. I shall describe what might be called the surface structure or semantic level of an experience as lived. Here I attend to the range of sensory evidence that accompanies seeing in our non-technological experience. I shall also consider the example in terms of what may be called its formal structure or syntactic level. This means focusing on formal features and modes of organization in the natural, lived experience and in the elaborations of that experience which are dependent upon our inventions, and constitute an unnatural experience. Lastly, I shall return to the question of value in connection with my students' difficulties with "abstract" texts, and correlate those difficulties to differences in how value is presented in lived, verbal, and video experience. The analysis thus moves from phenomenology to hermeneutics, from description of both content and form to interpretation of the role of formal features in presenting meaning.

Within natural lived experience, all vision is accompanied by a variety of contributions from our other senses as well as by constant subtle as well as obvious variations in visual display correlative to kinestheses. Let me first consider the latter factor. As I move across a windy bay in a kayak, I see the shore more clearly with every stroke of the paddle that succeeds in propelling the craft—and thus me—forward. But my lack of strength and skill is directly manifested by short and long spans of time in which that display changes more in a sideways direction than in depth. Rather than seeing the same section of shoreline, slightly larger, I see a different section of shoreline even though I haven't moved my eyes or head sideways. What I see tells me what I must do in order to stay on course and moving toward my destination. What I do is immediately apparent in what I see as well as in the signs of weariness: loss of physical power as I progress toward the shore, and shifts in the precise location of that weariness as I change strokes in order to steer.

In addition to these kinesthetic differences, changes in the visual display do not occur at a fixed distance from my body as they would if I were watching a film or television program in which the camera took the kayaker's-eye view. My foreground view of my own body, as paddler, appears against a changing background of the kayak in relation to the water, and the expanse of water in relation to the shore. However, the foreground view of my own body, as film or video viewer, is almost unrelated to the changing visual display. The "almost" here refers to the changes that can be effected by changing my posture or position in relation to the television screen; major changes of this sort are more difficult to bring about in a movie theater. (Although cinema and video are alike in that they both constitute technologically elaborated visual experience, they also differ in many ways. Thus, in order to limit the length of this analysis, the only technologically elaborated visual experience at issue is video experience.)

Quite obviously, a range of tactile and sensory experience is inevitable in lived experience and unavailable to video experience: the dampness of wind and spray against my skin, the peculiar taste of that spray, the varying chill as I turn my body in relation to the wind, the pressure of my knees against the kayak's shell, the constantly changing olfactory sensations from the shoreline in contrast to both the open water and the relatively faint scent of a shirt soaked by both water and my own perspiration. Sensory experience, such as the smell of the shoreline and the sound of birdcalls, is limited or augmented by mental and physical actions (e.g., turning my body and shifting my attention) as well as by changes in the wind, so that delineation of willed (internal) from imposed (external) sensations is uncertain.

Perhaps not quite so obviously, a range of affective experience is occasioned in the lived experience but present only in attentuated form, if at all, in the video experience. There are multiple pleasures and pains interweaving with kinesthesis and sentience in varying degrees as I anticipate the trip, push off at the start, persevere through its length, and finally climb onto the shore to rest in a warm and sheltered patch of sun. Nor do I fear overturning into water perhaps populated by sharks when I'm settled on the sofa to watch this kayak crossing on the television. Thus the tension that is all too palpable in my body actually crossing the bay is absent in that body as it enjoys the video experience. Also absent, when the passage is completed, is the relief, sense of accomplishment, and feeling of confidence in regard to future trips.

Perhaps the least obvious feature of this lived experience is its cognitive dimension, which contributes to the feelings of confidence and accomplishment. The decisions I make in anticipating and accomplishing this journey involve a great deal of reasoning. I draw strong and weak inductive conclusions, as well as make deductions, from both general knowledge (e.g., my strength and skill) and scientific data (e.g., water currents in relation to the land, wind velocity at different times of day, amount of daylight at this time of year in this location, etc.). Activities and strategies of both formal and informal logic—syllogistic reasoning, disjunction, conditionals, generalization, all of Mill's methods—are employed under circumstances that by contrast make a final exam appear leisurely. Thus, although I treat kayaking as "recreation," a variety of cognitive skills—construing, using, revising, and assessing ideas—are intrinsic to the very occurrence of the experience.

In contrast to this active and intense call upon my reasoning skills, rather different cognitive demands are involved in hearing or reading about this experience, and still others in watching it on television. Lived experience exercises what I call *reciprocal* reasoning, insofar as my reasoning influences the ongoing course of events and is in turn influenced by those events. I must, for instance, judge the strength of a gust of wind and combine that assessment with appropriate kinestheses if I am to stay afloat and even make progress toward the shore. Verbal and video experience, in contrast, demand what I would call *reconstructive* reasoning, structured in each case by their own formal features. In reconstructing an experience, I rely upon visual and verbal evidence that has a problematical relationship to the actual events as they were lived. The gust of wind just mentioned, for instance, would most likely be signaled on television by heightened music and cuts (rapid shifts of visual image) from the kayaker's face to rapidly developing waves of trees bending on the shore. A storyteller might well imitate the sound of the rising wind; but a story writer could only say that the wind increased, and perhaps transcribe the storyteller's imitation phonetically.

The last category of factors to consider is one which I believe to be closely tied to the intense exercise of cognitive skills in lived experience: Value here is continually assessed and reassessed as the relative importance and sheer number of factors entering into a lived reasoning process changes. *Value* now refers not only to factual importance, but also to strength and worth in the moral and aesthetic senses. Moral and aesthetic reasoning almost certainly are employed in the context that surrounds this passage across the bay, and may well enter also in reasoning about aspects of the crossing; for example, should I risk my own safety to help another kayaker who seems to be in danger? Should I have stayed at home to help paint a friend's house, rather than take this trip? Why is the view from this spot beautiful, the sound of that bird ugly? How is it that the kayak's shape is far more pleasing than, say, a rowboat's shape?

All of these dimensions of lived experience—kinesthetic, sensory (including aural, tactile, visual, gustatory, and olfactory), affective, cognitive, moral, aesthetic—in correlation, constitute that experience. I speak of them as the *formal features* of that experience because they can be analytically identified as the *invariant categories* into which the particular, varied content of a range of experiences may be sorted.[7] Even a segment of the sort of complex situation I described above, such as the lived experience of a gust of wind, exemplifies, in varying degrees, all of these formal features.[8] Thus, when I discuss and describe that experienced gust of wind as I have done here, I rely on the reader's possessing these structural features by virtue of his or her own comparable experiences.

In other words, the verbal presentation of this experience, whether spoken or written, may evoke—but cannot use—the formal features that serve to organize the lived experience. On the other hand, the verbal presentation uses formal features appropriate to itself and absent from the lived experience. On the sentence level, this means organization in terms of parts of speech (nouns, verbs, adjectives), parts of a sentence (phrases, clauses) and functional roles (subject, predicate). At the level of the paragraph and entire discourse, this requires organization in terms of statement, development, and resolution. Even more generally, the presence or absence of features such as point of view, story, and principle allow identification of the discourse or text by its type (expository, narrative, hortatory). Printed text, in contrast to spoken discourse, uses some visual forms in addition to those just listed, for example, the paragraph. However, it can only present certain formal features of spoken discourse in limited ways; for example, underlining or italics or boldface signifies emphasis, but in an impoverished way, compared to the vast range of nuance in speech. There is hardly any way to signify the almost constant changes in pace that characterize most speech, nor can the printed text signify the affective dimension that posture and gesture contribute to nontechnological spoken discourse. All of that must be described, rather than presented through structural features. Again, in telling the experience I use here an example, I rely on the anonymous reader's possession of those formal features.

Vision also relies on formal features that are peculiar to it, in contrast to those that serve to structure lived or verbal experience. I want to stress two qualifying factors before further consideration of video's formal features. First, although I mentioned vision, this analysis is limited to video visuality, which is a major limitation. Just as the paragraph is peculiar to printed text in contrast to spoken discourse, other formal fea-

tures serve to structure other sorts of visual presentation such as natural
(nontechnologically elaborated) seeing, paintings, and highway signs.[9]
Also, my identification of invariant structures peculiar to different sorts
of experience—structures that both present particular content and organize lived, verbal, and visual experience—is a matter of description and
interpretation, rather than evaluation. This reminder seems to be especially pertinent in studying the formal features of video because this particular mode of experience is the focus of a perhaps unprecedented
amount of criticism at this time.[10]

In order to focus on the formal features of video, let us first use
just a segment of the lived experience of crossing that windy bay. The
video image of experiencing an especially windy spell would probably
rely upon augmenting the natural sound through amplification and/or
evocative musical background. It could, but need not, retain the temporal ordering of segments within lived experience, but it would do so
through technologically developed means other than the natural tactile,
olfactory, and visual sensations that provide that structure in lived experience. For example, the rising wind would plaster my damp shirt
against my body, and I could feel that without looking at it. The video
image might cut or zoom in to the shirt; if the dampness were not
enough to show, extra water would be applied (off camera, of course) so
that this aspect might be translated from the tactile to the visual dimension. In order to signify that a change of wind makes me aware of birds'
cries, even though their actual intensity is no greater, the noise could be
amplified. On the other hand, if the wind shift brought olfactory evidence of the shore into my awareness, that might be visually signified by
cutting or zooming to birds walking along the driftwood on shore. My
anxiety at keeping the craft upright could be suggested by cutting rapidly
from my face to the waves and back again, even though I am actually
more likely to be looking steadily at the shore. Also, I might be shown
wiping perspiration from my brow, even though, in actuality, the wind
would dry whatever perspiration appeared too rapidly for me to do so.
(Here again, the off-camera wet sponge might supply what nature de-
nies.) Rapid panning from face to hands and intense gripping of the
paddle could signify increased mental and physical effort. Inserting images of me in the kayak, taken from a distance ahead, behind, beside, or
above would serve to unify these intrinsically disparate parts into a
whole. However, I could not experience myself from those viewpoints,
and so the whole that is constructed is one accessible to the video

viewer, but not to me as instigator of and participant in the experience.

And what about a consideration of the whole, in other words, the entire experience of crossing the bay? Although video could simply depict this whole exactly in the manner it was lived, from a single perspective and in the same amount of time, such an approach is rarely ever used. I doubt that even I, who lived the experience, could maintain interest through watching a full-length videotape taken from a camera mounted, say, immediately behind my shoulder. Such a point is so obvious that we usually would not stop to think why two hours of crossing a bay, with viewpoint limited by a natural field of vision and audio accompaniment limited to the natural features of the environment, is thoroughly entertaining, while a videotaped version of the same experience would be dreadfully boring.

Although this segment of lived experience (considering now the entire crossing as one segment within my life) is anything but boring, not all of lived experience is equally captivating. Video experience avoids the dull end of the interest spectrum characteristic of lived experience by employing formal features—compression, ellipsis, inserts, montage—which function to sustain viewers' interest. These are adaptations of features that serve the same function in verbal experience; they differ from features noted earlier in that they do not serve to translate a tactile event, for instance, into a spatial, externally visible one. Rather, they alter the pace of lived experience, while preserving the sense of both lived experience's continuity and video experience's depictive character. I will return to this point in discussing contrasts in typical assessment of video, verbal, and lived experience.

Although I could continue to describe likely features of a video translation of this lived experience, I hope that these examples suffice to make the point, namely, that this translation, like all translation, requires replacing one structure with another. In some exercises, such as in translating from German to English, the structures involved are quite similar. In others, such as in my telling of this experience in contrast to my living it, the differences are substantial. Furthermore, reflection reveals two major differences between translating into verbal experience and translating into video experience. First, it is obvious that the story told in conversation or on the page is quite a different experience from the lived occurrence. The video experience, however, typically purports to be a depiction, rather than a portrayal; that is, it simulates the lived experience by translating as much as possible of that experience into one formed by its own structure. As with all structures, we habitually use this one without examining it. But when I do reflect upon it, I discover that the syntax of video as a visual experience is spatial and temporal.[11] Whatever cannot be translated from the kinesthetic, sensory (including aural, tactile, visual, gustatory, and olfactory), affective, cognitive, moral, and aesthetic structures of lived experience, into spatial or temporal forms, must be omitted.[12] Viewers who are video-literate understand these translations, just as those who are print-literate understand that words underlined in dialogue signify that the speaker emphasized those words.

The second major difference between translating from lived into video experience, in contrast to translating into verbal experience, has to do with typical perception of the video experience. Despite its simplified structure, video is typically perceived as "realistic" and "informative," in other words, as providing a depiction that expands our knowledge of the real world rather than limiting it.[13] As I noted early in this consideration, technologically elaborated vision can indeed see what is too far or too small to be seen naturally, as well as what cannot be seen naturally, that is, the sight of ourselves in a range of activities. More information is given, at the cost of what I would call depth or texture, for only that sensory evidence which can be seen or heard is retained in the translated experience. Although no listener or reader would mistake my verbal portrayal of a kayaking adventure as "the real thing," or judge that the verbal presentation is a fair substitute for living the experience, just those assessments are typically made in regard to video experience.

There is a great deal more to be said about how the formal features of each mode of experience focus attention, facilitate comprehension, and indeed constitute meaningfulness. I hope, however, that this brief consideration of the different structures in these types of experience will support some tentative conclusions. A brief review of those issues may be helpful before drawing those conclusions. First, Paul Goldberger's remarks on the lack of "inherent substance" in much contemporary cultural production suggested to me that the video text, by virtue of its formal structure—and thus in distinction from the programming which is that text's content—disinherits the sort of meaningfulness that is, for us, foundational for recognizing and assessing value.

I then turned to my own teaching experience in order to elaborate on that meaningfulness as a function of a particular sort of reasoning, which I call *interpretive* in contrast to *explanatory* reasoning. The former involves associating *conclusions* with *reasons;* that is, understanding a paragraph or even an entire essay as a connected series of descriptions and assertions, some of which are offered as evidence, support, or reason for others. In order to do this, we must focus on the *ideas* and viewpoint presented in a *text,* rather than on the *opinions* or psychological standpoint of an *author.* However, students typically explain a conclusion as the effect of a psychological motivation that functions, more or less, like a physical cause. What is almost entirely absent in this explanatory reasoning is the ability, disposition, or skill that enables understanding a conclusion on the basis of the argument that leads up to it.

The final aspect of this study required taking an experience of my own as an example in order to thematize its structure as a *lived* experience, as recounted *verbally,* and as it might be represented in a *video* text. The general hypothesis underlying this example is that interpretive reasoning, which discovers and explores ideas so as to reach understanding, is an established habit—at least for those who display particular affinities for the printed word, and that would include, I expect, architecture critics and teachers in the humanities. What reflection on the example may reveal is that we do this in lived experience as well as in verbal and video experience. Although the formal features available to those two modes of experience are quite different, each mode displays intentional activity appropriate to constituting meaningfulness within the restrictions of that experience's formal structure. Also, as reflection reveals, typically we do not hesitate to translate lived into verbal experience. In the absence of formal features that allow kinesthetic and tactile evidence, verbal experience, quite appropriately and almost always without notice, exploits those structures *intrinsic to it.*

Furthermore, the limitations of verbal experience typically are not judged as limitations in the development and practice of cognitive skills, and in particular, in constituting meaningfulness and recognizing value. This seems odd, once we notice that it is only in lived experience that the actual outcome depends upon our exercising those skills. This is to say that both video and verbal experience demand that we *reason,* in order to accomplish the task. Yet, curiously, it is only television, not reading books and not even conversation, which is typically judged as *passive* entertainment—albeit, one that can also supply a good deal of information and can expand our horizons in a comparatively effortless way, compared to lived and verbal experience.

However, I would argue that both aspects of that judgment are mistaken. For all three modes of experience are alike in requiring us to exploit their formal structures in order to constitute (i.e., make sense of) the available evidence. The differences in the results of those activities are thus differences in *intentionality*: that is, differences in how the available affective, cognitive, kinesthetic, and sensory evidence is used to actualize a correlation with what is experienced, in these different modes of experiencing.

On the basis of their differences in formal features, I find that these three modes of experience provide three distinct sorts of *presentations*, rather than verbal and video experience providing *representations* of lived experience. The perceived lack of "intrinsic substance," meaningfulness, and value in cultural production structured by, or influenced by, video experience may then be, instead, a lack of that substance, meaningfulness, and value which depend on lived and verbal experience. For lived experience forces us to develop gradations of importance in the multitude of judgments necessary to bring a task to completion, such as accomplishing the crossing of a windy bay in a kayak. The verbal presentation of that crossing allows us to enjoy that accomplishment vicariously only through *imaginative* exertion comparable to the physical exertion of the actual crossing. Because of the highly impoverished evidence allowed by the formal features of verbal experience (and the printed word, as noted earlier, is far more impoverished of evidence than the spoken), we must constitute in imagination what lived experience constituted in the actual event. Metaphorically, this requires an imaginative skill and muscle, comparable to the physical skill and muscle that was required in the actual experience. A multitude of judgments, which become habitual, are needed in both cases.

In the video experience as well as in the verbal, what is experienced depends upon the form as well as the content. We are mistaken in considering the result as a copy of lived experience, just as some philosophers and critics, in my judgment, have been mistaken in thinking of verbal experience and visual art as copies of lived experience. The form of video experience is impoverished in some of the same ways as that of verbal experience. Nevertheless, I would argue that we are more easily misled into considering the video image as an icon, that is, as a *pictorial representation* of *lived experience*. In short, I argue that we are mistaken in our understanding of the structures of video intentionality to the extent that we analyze it in terms of a replication—and usually, as an inferior replication—of lived or verbal intentionality. Also, even this preliminary consideration of the difference in syntax between lived and video experience suggests that the resulting products or "intentional objects" must be quite different in each instance. The form of video is limited to spatial and temporal presentation, and whatever "inherent substance" cannot be depicted or portrayed through those means, will not be communicated and will, therefore, remain foreign to the structures of video intentionality.

We who are habituated to verbal experience (both spoken and written) believe, however, that we are able to constitute meaningfulness and value from that experience, comparable to what is constituted in lived experience. Is it possible that we are mistaken as to the comparability of these two domains of meaning and value? It is certainly the case that intellectual history, going back to Plato, records our adherence to a copy theory of linguistic presentation. In its thoroughly Platonic version, this requires adopting the Platonic Forms as the most valued experience, objects in lived experience as (so to speak) second-rate, and artistic objects (whether verbal or visual) as third-rate. In the modified Platonism that, I believe, surfaces in much contemporary criticism of contemporary culture in general and media in particular, linguistic objects are the most valued.[14] Given our habituation to, and even veneration of, written texts, we may be oblivious to the distinctive meaningfulness and value intrinsic to both lived and video experience. In theory, at least, more homage is paid to the former than to the latter, but that may be nothing more than a vestige of the Platonism embedded in the verbal culture we inhabit. We bring no such vestige to video experience and this is, perhaps, its greatest promise.

I do not claim to know whether, or how, the formal features of video experience should or could support that interpretive reasoning which seems to be the condition for traditional meaningfulness and value judgment. Nevertheless, it seems to me that video's reliance on spatiotemporal structure contributes to the practice of constituting cause-and-effect meaningfulness in very simple, even simplistic, ways. I find this increasingly reflected in student reliance on the explanatory modes of reasoning described earlier. Although we bookish people may be misguided in thinking so, we typically believe that our verbal experience translates the meaningfulness and values of lived experience in a much more substantive way, and that it may even constitute cognitive and affective meaningfulness and value of its own. Familiarity with, and even habituation to, both those modes may well obscure the considerable effort required to translate between them adequately. Familiarity may also obscure the differences between them. Focusing on the syntax of all three modes of experience is, I hope, a first step toward considering whether, and how, a correlative translation should and could be made into video experience.[15]

– 5 –

The Electronic Golden Calf

Gregor Goethals

Most American commercial television is entertainment and its primary source of revenue is advertising—the numberless commercials which effervesce periodically throughout the broadcasting day. Yet we only need look briefly at various programs and commercials to recognize authoritative images that embody the mythology of the American Way.

In other historical settings symbolic representations have been pervasive, appearing in a great variety of visual forms: metalwork and jewelry, ceramics, glass, painting, and sculpture. These mythological subjects, however, knew none of the boundaries we draw today between "high art" and "craft." Homeric heroes and gods—Achilles, Ajax, Zeus, Apollo, and Aphrodite—were found on vases and lamps as well as in temple relief sculpture. In cultures where myths were less anthropomorphic, totemic motifs appeared on dishes, weapons, fishhooks, and clothing. Today, in some contemporary nonwestern societies popular images of heroes and deities appear in great variety in everyday contexts. In North India, for example, the venerated Rama may be depicted on the side of a truck, or one may hear a recitation of his deeds on an audiocassette. And now television has portrayed the great *Ramayana* epic. Pious viewers wrap the TV set with garlands of flowers to celebrate the images that flow across the screen.[1]

In our secular society we may speculate about the symbolic power and authority of the serialized narratives of soap operas, sitcoms, and dramas, as well as the mythology of news, sports, political telecasts, and commercials. The totality portrays an assortment of values that we associate with the American way of life. The range of TV programming may be seen as a mythological reservoir with national and international ramifications.

Tales of the Good Life

Several critics of the media have adapted the concept of "myth," using its anthropological and sociological meanings to shed light on the broader functions of television in American culture. British critic Roger Silverstone suggests that television mythology expresses "a need and a constraint." Even secular societies depend upon stories to communicate shared meanings and to set limits as to what is socially acceptable. As Homeric myths identified common loyalties and set boundaries for the Hellenes, so popular art forms today witness to collective world-views and portray current heroes and antiheroes.

Television tells stories that are readily identifiable and offer reassurance; they provide "something of the elementary, the primary, the fundamental and stable."[2] Without some commonly accepted narratives that articulate the truths and falsehoods, the values and disvalues of a culture, we would find life intolerably disorienting. In this sense television's entertainment programs may speak to a human need for identity, both individual and social. As to the constraints of popular mythology, Silverstone points out that the mythic "worlds" that television constructs within the real world may operate in a conservative and restraining way, politically, socially, and economically. Conflicts and resolutions narrated in the popular mythology of television tend to reinforce existing institutions. While traditional myths and rituals provided some opportunities for identifiable change, the modifications of contemporary values and institutions brought about through television are less clear.[3] One cannot measure the actual effects of television upon viewers and can never be sure what people make of the things they hear and see. Still it is important to analyze the medium's narratives and symbols.

Many critics contend that in TV mythology there is little concern for public good, and general contentment with the existing institutional order. The familiar images, for example, that open the program "Dallas" set the stage for the characters' persistent drive for money and control: the cityscape with its skyline of corporate headquarters, the stately ranch compound of the Ewing family, oil rigs silhouetted against the horizon, and heroic images of cowboys rounding up a massive herd of cattle. In their various roles as businessmen, worldwide oil speculators, and ranchers, the Ewing brothers, as well as their adversaries, constantly struggle to acquire and to dominate. Only in his role of father does J. R. seem to soften and momentarily modify his preoccupation with success and power.

One can, nevertheless, point to a few shows whose mythological characters offer other perspectives on the good life. Some of these focus on the kinds of changes that are supposedly occurring in American society. Gloria Steinem wrote a brief article for *TV Guide* describing "Cagney and Lacey" as the best show on television,[4] and those who have followed the series since it began in 1982 have recognized a different kind of symbolic representation. Here are two women whose lives are shown largely outside the home as they carry out their professional commitments. Early fans saw these women as new heroines in their role as policewomen, giving a different twist to the genre of police dramas. The domestic status of each—one happily married, the other single—was a secondary, minor motif. Steinem notes that the series represents a departure from the trivial assumptions that women cannot get along and that they are essentially a part of a man's world, rivaling each other for his affections. In earlier shows, the relationship between women was usually comic; for example, Lucy Ricardo and Ethel Mertz in "I Love Lucy." She contrasts the friendship of Cagney and Lacey with that in another contemporary story about two women, "Kate and Allie." Here, however, Steinem comments that, since the two women are without men, they are defined as "victims." On the other hand, the relationship between Cagney and Lacey depends not on their relationships to men but on their common professional work as policewomen.

The show has been applauded not only for the role models it presents, but also for the daring presentation of themes that bring controversial topics into public discourse. Departing from screeching tires and shootouts, "Cagney and Lacey" may be compared to another highly respected show from earlier seasons, "Hill Street Blues." Both have dealt with highly sensitive issues that seldom appear on television: alcoholism, abortion, and date rape. Many critics have applauded the moving portrayal by Sharon Gless as Cagney, facing a potential problem with alcohol. After her alcoholic father dies following a fall in his apartment, a wake is held in Flannery's Bar. The bereft daughter repeatedly toasts his memory with drinks. Recalling other episodes in which Lacey has gently chided Cagney about her drinking, viewers have an uneasy feeling that alcoholism is a potential threat for her.

The show also received praises for giving alternative images of marriage and family. Lacey's husband, Harvey, is a blue-collar worker married to an independent woman following a nontraditional profession. Viewers also see a policewoman as mother. Lacey takes a maternity leave from the force to have her third child. In one program Lacey, about to deliver at any moment, resumes her role as policewoman in tracking down a hit-and-run driver. Harvey, concerned about her condition, joins Cagney in the detective work while Lacey orchestrates the search from their Queens apartment. Later we see the tensions that arise over the care of children when both parents work, as Harvey and Lacey deal with parenting and family responsibility. Although the themes explored in "Cagney and Lacey" have a harsher ring than those of "The Cosby Show," for example, they too are mythic in that they provide tangible symbols for changing expectations of women and of thinking about women. Even when conflicts are not resolved, as in the issue of abortion, alternative views, through their symbolization in this powerful medium, become more comprehensible.

Since mythic authority asserts itself through repeated stories, soap operas play a unique role in our culture. Here are daily, continuous patterns of tales that entertain while they dramatize social dynamics and role models. For an hour or more, soap operas move slowly, almost dully (like real life), through conflicts and tensions. While usually comfortably middle class, these heroes and heroines, frequently employed as doctors and lawyers, engage endlessly in conversations and crises: intrigue, infidelity, surgery, nervous breakdowns, having children or deciding not to have them, running away, making up, terminal illness, getting married, getting divorced, separation, death, abortion, alcoholism, and amnesia. Human relationships and the value decisions that radiate from them are the stuff of soap operas. Their slow pace and the relatively constant cast of performers enable viewers to keep up with the stories, even if one or two episodes are missed. For avid fans *Soap Opera Digest* is published weekly, with its reviews of previous programs and its articles that speculate on future events and decisions that leading characters may make and the effects on their lives. Like fanciful tales and gossip that surround political, religious, or cultural dignitaries, these webs of fantasy confer an almost lifelike quality on fictional heroes and heroines of the daytime dramas. Through their prolonged daily exposure, fictional characters become surrogate household members and provide common bonds among those who watch the same soap opera.

The morality plays of "soaps" dramatize the interaction between good and evil in easily understood terms. Unlike traditional myths, however, they do not resolve conflicts in a single episode. Rather, they are openended, more like life itself. The viewer moves with the characters through their lives and changing circumstances. In long-running shows, such as "All My Children," changing social attitudes are reflected in the characters and their human problems. In recent years daytime dramas have portrayed increased sexual freedom, and several have dealt with the topic of homosexuality. As the AIDS phenomenon erupted in real life, some soaps introduced this into their make-believe tragedies. Working their way slowly through time, these lifelike melodramas, at once ordinary and extraordinary, provide a constant audiovisual hum of moral tales every weekday afternoon. After weeks, sometimes months, in the end, the good prevails, pausing only momentarily in triumph before the shadows of evil appear again. These leisurely everyday dramas take us through a moral meandering over an indefinite span of time and, as in life, the resolutions are tentative and fragile.

In contrast to soap operas, another type of mythic tale, the commercial, telescopes and compresses decision and action into a few brief seconds. Terse, fast-action sequences about things the advertiser wants viewers to need or desire constitute its basic structure. Although viewers may disdain them, they provide the networks with their basic revenue. They have become an integral part of most broadcasting in the United States, permeating all kinds of programs. Minidramas about "the good life," the commercials draw from a wide range of themes: good fellowship and friendship, warm family ties and loving relationships between parents and children, success in professional life, pride in personal looks and the anticipation of constant improvement, the accumulation of possessions for comfort and for the minimization of work, the achievement of social status, the enhancement of personal growth and performance, patriotism and pride in community, the privilege of choice and the positive values of competition. These motifs are frequently combined with national celebrations, conventional holidays, and sports events.

In 1988 McDonalds aired a commercial related to the Olympics which brought out contrasting values and emotions that may be experienced in highly competitive events. It portrayed, in fact, the anxieties and disappointments of losing. Having failed in his attempt to qualify for the international games, a young athlete is shown as he returns to his hometown, not in triumph but with a sense of defeat. On the trip homeward he broods about failed expectations and how he will face family and friends. In split seconds the mood of the commercial dramatically changes. Waiting for him at the station are family, relatives, and friends with open arms. They greet and embrace him as though he were returning from a heroic victory. Here is a special moral tale of the good life: Family and friends transform defeat into celebration of the person. Competition is overshadowed by the supportive love and nurturing of a community of caring individuals. It is, of course, McDonalds that reminds us of these redemptive values and links its product to them. This giant fast-food corporation is not alone, however, in recognizing the powerful symbols embedded in images of the family.

From modestly designed ads in small newspapers to high-tech video commercials, advertising reaffirms the values we associate with the good life and reassures us that these are constant and obtainable. Advertising, like the older church- or state-sponsored art, celebrates and eulogizes the system that subsidizes it. Commercials, sitcoms, and soaps imaginatively visualize what we find worthy or unworthy, yet we regard these as *make-believe*, while other TV images are described as real. For instance, many viewers accept the news programs as a way of finding out what's happening in the world. Yet these, too, are symbolic and selective, revealing what our society values and disvalues.

Shaping Reality

"What's going on?" is an essentially human question. Throughout time it has been asked wherever life is shared, in the family, neighborhood, city, and nation. Today television enables the question to be raised throughout the universe. TV sets may bring into individual homes audiovisual reports of what's going on around the world, as well as in space. As McLuhan and others anticipated, the information revolutions—both print and electronic—have transformed our sense of community *and* our perspectives of reality. Within hours, sometimes minutes, we have sights and sounds of events in distant places which may evoke fear, anguish, sympathy, and responsive action. In pre-modern times religious and political leaders were careful to select the events that were publicly proclaimed, events that affected the lives of everyone. These were memorialized on architectural forms in carved and painted images. In the classical world, for example, important military victories were narrated on columns and triumphal arches as well as on temples.

Throughout the history of the United States public access to information and the right to free speech and press enabled news institutions to assume the responsibility for giving open answers to the question: "What's going on?" Moreover, the role of newspapers became increasingly important as the population of the country grew more religiously, racially, and ethnically complex. In the nineteenth century Alexis de Toqueville recognized the ways in which newspapers became a unifying, symbolizing agent. In contrast to their role in aristocracies, newspapers are particularly vital to democracies. They become the source of shared knowledge and can identify common interests and needs for action. Without knowing each other, strangers may talk every day and make decisions without ever meeting. "The newspaper," wrote this French observer of American society, "comes of its own accord and talks to you briefly everyday on the common weal, without distracting you from your private affairs." He compares the newspaper to a beacon which unites wandering minds. "Only a newspaper," he said, can "drop the same thought into a thousand minds at the same moment."⁵

Written over 150 years ago, these remarks are equally useful today in pointing out the authoritative role of news agencies in fabricating our collective symbols of reality. Reading on a crowded subway or bus, picking up the paper from the mailbox in an isolated rural area, or turning on the TV newscasts are actions that link Americans with one another. In this respect, television is especially powerful. As persons watch the news, they are aware that others are also watching and that there will be common subjects and events to discuss. Shared perceptions draw separate individuals into a fragile and illusory order which otherwise would not exist. Amid fragmented constituencies—religious, political, and economic—the mass media attempt to portray significant events and provide information that enables us to understand ourselves and this complex society.

The nightly news programs, for example, present accounts of reality, carefully constructed narratives made up of both words and images that explain what is happening in the world. The success of television's ritualistic orientation may be measured by the fact that most of us do not view the news as a symbolic construction but as an essentially believable reality. It has been argued, however, that the system is not so open as it should be; that is, what we see, or more important, what we don't see distorts reality. The precise effects of press coverage are not easily determined, but we can examine more closely its power to select the issues that are publicly represented and discussed. Several critics have claimed that the mass media, especially television, promote an illusory perception of reality and tend to generate uniformity of opinion. The selective presentation of information limits, even manipulates, public debate.

To consider these issues we need to look at television as a symbolizing process: first, the selection involved in camerawork and editing, and second, the composition of diverse portions of news footage into a carefully fabricated whole. The creation of images in all media—painting, photography, sculpture, graphic arts—is essentially a selective process. None of the visual arts, including television, can present reality. Instead they all represent experience, selecting certain things to emphasize while ignoring many others. Yet photography, film, and particularly television appear to have a special claim on authenticity. In a portrait or landscape painting we may, of course, recognize the subject; but however "lifelike" the image, the hand of the creator is evident. Whether we are looking at a contemporary neorealist or fifteenth-century Flemish work, we can observe how the artist works to give the impression of a human face or figure. Separating the reality of the person and the image itself are the painter's brushstrokes and pigments, and we accept the fact that the artist has revealed certain things and veiled others. Most viewers presume the presence of the artist as mediator, negotiating reality for us through the form.

Photography, film, and television, by contrast, appear to unveil material existence and join viewers in a one-to-one relationship to it. The presence of the mediator is not so readily detected. These media seem to be more "objective." We assume that camera lenses, like our own, are transparent agents through which the world yields its palpable truths. The analogy between human and mechanical lenses helps to support the notion that these media are innocent observers that capture reality as it unfolds. Since film and television involve moving images, we find even stronger associations between image and experience. To comprehend the authoritative power of news programs we need to be conscious of the creative, selective process involved in the re-presentation of events that flow across the TV screen. Images that seem to put us directly in touch with distant places and events are there because technical and editorial control has been exerted at several levels.

To give one example, in the fall of 1988, respected TV anchorperson Ted Koppel raised the question of why American TV covers the Third World as it does. Discussing this issue with him were Ambassador Oumarou Youssouffou, from the Organization of African Unity; Lawrence Grossman, former president of NBC News; and Alexander Cockburn, writer for the *Wall Street Journal* and the *Nation*. Ambassador Youssouffou offered several illustrations of the problem. He noted that the condor egg in California received as much or more reporting than a continent of 400 million people. Even the tragic events and loss of life in Burundi, Mozambique, and Ethiopia seemed of little interest to the viewing public. He was especially concerned about racist overtones, pointing to the prominent attention given to violence against whites, as contrasted to the underreporting of assaults upon nonwhites. While what happens to a white farmer in Mozambique or South Africa becomes front-page news he observed, it takes a massive massacre of blacks to get comparable reporting.

Both Grossman and Cockburn agreed with Koppel's assessment that today there is even less coverage of the Third World than there was ten years ago. Lawrence Grossman commented that there are NBC news bureaus and correspondents in all the major capitals of Western Europe, yet only one NBC correspondent in Africa—in South Africa—and none in South America. He noted also that even editors and professional journalists have little historical or other knowledge about many of these remote, yet important, places. The general public, moreover, appears both uninformed and uninterested. Alexander Cockburn added that TV news programs, and to an extent the press in general, have become forms of entertainment, rather than information.

Cockburn brought up the role of government in determining news coverage. The agenda of the president or the State Department enables certain parts of the world to leap into prominence and then vanish from the headlines, and frequently from public concern. Our shifting political and diplomatic ventures in Southeast Asia, Central and South America, and Afghanistan draw attention to particular places and events. One country may be featured prominently for weeks, even months, and then completely disappear from the news. In his final remarks Cockburn suggested that with the easing of tensions between the Soviet Union and the United States the reporting of Third World people and events might move in new directions, such as their economies and world ecology.

Cockburn also made the point that TV news is presented in symbolic terms, a concept which a number of critics have pursued. In her book, *Making News*, Gaye Tuchman, for example, describes news as a "web of facticity." But rather than representing society and its social structures, newspersons and institutions actively create symbolic world views. These serve as a "window on the world" through which news consumers perceive reality. She asks: Who creates these windows and where are they placed? Does a window have many panes or few? Are they clear or opaque? Since worlds of private and communal experience are, in fact, almost limitless in number, which ones are selected to be disclosed? The essence of the newswindows, Tuchman concludes, is their capacity to symbolize and to set limits on what is perceived as the "real" world.[6]

The disclosure, for example, of the Poindexter disinformation campaign in 1986 evoked criticism from both conservative and liberal commentators who objected to the government's abuse of the American press. Most argued that the freedom of free press in the United States depends upon the credibility of information from the government. Discussion of Poindexter's tactics was cut short by even more shocking revelations of the Iran-Contra scandal, again traced to the President's national security advisors. These latter disclosures would momentarily deface the trustworthy, "take-charge" portrait of Ronald Reagan. To counter the image-making power of news institutions, media experts in the White House now specialize in political portraiture, which has become indispensable for the communication of political authority.

This use of visual symbols to enhance the position of rulers and politicians is not new. Throughout history heads of empires and states have employed visual artists to create symbols of authority that depict the order they represent and uphold. The communications revolution has brought images in different forms but their function has remained the same: to render visible and thus objectify the invisible values that characterize a community and its leadership. Television is indispensable today to those who seek and would maintain political power.

Iconified Politics

Emperors and politicians of the classical world, rulers of the early medieval church-states, and later European monarchs were variously portrayed as symbols of authority. Athens and Rome were filled with statues of famous leaders, while rulers of the Holy Roman Empire developed similar images. One example from the sixth century is particularly impressive, a mosaic depicting the Emperor Justinian, head of both church and empire, in the sanctuary of San Vitale, Ravenna. There, with ecclesiastical leaders to his left and civil servants and soldiers to his right, he stands as the supreme earthly ruler and highest priestly power.

As we examine contemporary symbols of authority we shall ask: How do politicians in a technological, democratic, and secular society use images to enhance their position? The media for modern political portraiture are not paint, stone, and mosaics but photography, film, and especially television. As politicians began to grasp the potential of television to reach millions of viewers and voters, the production of modern images of power rose dramatically. Our contemporary leaders are now portrayed on a scale comparable to the rulers of the ancient world. Replacing the sculptors, stonecutters, and painters today are publicity firms, media managers, and TV journalists. During the twentieth century, communication technologies have enabled politicians to establish a sense of their presence instantaneously. In the 1930s Franklin D. Roosevelt used radio to transcend barriers of time and space, becoming a "live" voice in family homes throughout the nation. John F. Kennedy was the first American president to benefit from television's capacity to draw viewers into the innermost spaces of political rites in which they immediately "participated" by seeing and hearing. In contrast, the loyal supporters of earlier rulers had only static images that retold ceremonial events. Today the television medium both presents and represents events even as they happen, creating a unique kind of authoritative image. Seated behind his desk in the Oval Office Ronald Reagan presented his farewell to the nation. He spoke of the revolution he had initiated. One of its greatest accomplishments, he said, was the rediscovery of our values and the restoration of national pride and patriotism. He warned that a loss of the "American memory" would result in an erosion of the country's spirit. "If we forget what we did, we won't know who we are." Our spirit is back, he asserted, but it must be reinstitutionalized. To accomplish this we need to pay more attention to American history, focusing not on fashion but on what is important. We should, he proposed, put "greater emphasis on civic ritual." Finally, he observed that all great changes begin at the family dinner table where parents talk to their children about what it means to be an American. Earlier in our national life patriotism was expressed in the family, in the neighborhood and in popular culture. That must happen again, said the president. In closing, the chief executive credited the success of his value revolution to "you the people." Reagan's regiments are the decent, ordinary citizens who supported him and restored faith and confidence in the nation's ideals.

The accomplishments of Reagan's regiments, however, would not be possible without the medium of television and the movie actor/politician's masterly understanding and practice of "civic ritual." Reagan and his aides deliberately found ways to ritualize events and to construct pervasive, moving images of authority. In a religiously plural, or for some, a secular society, many of the "photo opportunities" became occasions for civic rituals, means through which Reagan's media experts sought to manipulate the minds and hearts of viewers.

In an article for *TV Guide*[7] the president reflected on the privilege of seeing the depth and richness of the land and its people. We have, he said, shared in its celebrations and have spoken with and held those who have known great tragedy. These were occasions in which the faith and hope that seem uniquely American found new definition. He cited the national rejoicing as we celebrated the 100th birthday of the Statue of Liberty. Viewers may remember the dramatic pictures of the president as he relighted the torch of liberty. While he stood there in the summer night, the sky exploded with fireworks and Ronald Reagan seemed the embodiment of the strength and courage of the nation.

In the article the president also referred to one of the saddest events in the recent life of the country: the death of the Challenger astronauts. Since the live telecast landings on the moon in the 1970s, the United States had enjoyed spectacular success in creating positive, exciting pictures of adventures in space. For over a decade Americans watched exhilarating take-offs and landings. Space exploration seemed as natural for Americans as the pioneering of the great western plains and the conquest of the Rocky Mountains. The Challenger flight was to carry a New Hampshire schoolteacher into space, and journalists were competing for a place on the next space flight. On the morning of 28 January 1986, all communications media in the United States concentrated on the most tragic accident in the nation's prestigious space program. Within two minutes of lift-off from Cape Canaveral, Florida, the shuttle exploded and seven astronauts perished. The nation was in shock.

Through radio Ronald Reagan began to comfort the families, friends, colleagues—and the entire nation. Later during televised services at the Space Center in Houston, Texas, he officiated as priest, pastor, leader, friend. Viewers saw President and Mrs. Reagan moving amid the bereaved families, reaching out to them, comforting them. The memorial ceremony was presented by the major networks as an inclusive service for a grieving nation. The networks extended the coverage, drawing in mourners at other sites. In a temple in Akron, Ohio, a congregation held a service for Judith Resnick. In North Carolina Jesse Jackson was present at the church honoring Ronald McNair. Many people had gathered at the Space Museum in Washington, D.C. to express their sorrow and watch the president as he led the ceremony of lamentation.

As Reagan left office, his critics and supporters were almost unanimous about one thing: he made Americans feel good about themselves. Throughout his presidency, he underscored the traditional values of freedom, family, and patriotism. Both at home and abroad he articulated faith and confidence in the nation and its citizens. While long-range historical assessments proceed, there is little doubt that the fabrication of political icons to communicate ideology and leadership will continue. The 1988 conventions and presidential campaign underscored their primacy.

In the clash of symbols George Bush was clearly the winner. Much of the success of his campaign can be credited to the design and transformation of his image by his strategists. Standing in the background while a swashbuckling Reagan mesmerized the public, Bush appeared to be a wimpy yes-man. He emerged, however, from his 1988 P.R.-cocoon as a preppy Rambo, charging forth amid unfurled flags, using the same *we* versus *they* slogans that had worked so well for the Great Communicator.

Signs of the new Bush first appeared in January 1988, when he locked horns with Dan Rather, the famous CBS anchorperson. During a live interview on the evening news, Bush accused Rather of misleading him about the nature of the interview and for about twenty minutes they engaged in a sparring match for all to see. In retrospect this encounter was more lively than his debates with Dukakis. Bush's metamorphosis had been clearly evident in his early New Hampshire campaign against Robert Dole. Having lost in Iowa and behind in the polls, Bush and his advisors decided at the last minute on a negative advertisement against Dole. Labeled "Senator Straddle," it showed the senator from Kansas as indecisive, sidestepping, and equivocating, especially on taxes. Since Bush's organization had bought up all the available 30-second spots through the election day, Dole had no opportunity to respond on TV. Bush won New Hampshire.

In planning the fall campaign against the Democrats, Bush's media managers early in the summer of 1988 employed a marketing f·m. In an attempt to get a reading of attitudes, for 25 dollars each, it b·ought together persons who knew little about either Bush or Dukakis talk about the candidates:

> The moderator began asking rhetorical questions. "What if I told you that Dukakis vetoed a bill requiring schoolchildren to say the Pledge of Allegiance? Or that he was against the death penalty? Or that he gave weekend furloughs to first-degree murderers?" "He's a liberal!" exclaimed one man at the table. "If those are really his positions," a woman added, "I'd have a hard time supporting him."[8]

These groups were observed by Bush's team of image experts through a two-way mirror. From such experimentation and testing of public sentiments evolved some of the most persuasive political messages in many years.

The thread running through all the anti-Dukakis ads was the inflammatory, derogatory use of the word *liberal*. In the course of the campaign it became a dirty word, synonymous with "Communist," "traitor," "deviant." The famous "L" word was elaborated visually in many ways. Most publicized was a television commercial that called attention to the case of Willie Horton, a convicted black murderer, who raped a New Jersey woman while on prison furlough. In another instance Bush's ad team mocked Dukakis's attitude toward defense. They turned a news clip into a sensational caricature. Trying to build his image as a man strong on military matters, the Democratic candidate took a few turns around a field in a tank, and this appeared on the nightly news. The pictures of a small helmeted head peering uncomfortably from a gigantic armored vehicle became the centerpiece for a Bush ad that highlighted the awkward, indeed comic, look of the governor of Massachusetts in military gear. Whether or not George Bush was uncomfortable with the negative dimensions of his advertising strategy and his new persona, he nevertheless continued on this course through the campaign.

Immediately after his November victory Bush's media portraitists went to work to sketch another George. The lean, mean, shoot-from-the-hip campaigner was restyled for stately leadership. Brushstrokes, that is, film clips of a relaxed family man reaching out a friendly hand to his opponents, covered up the blemishes of the campaign. The viewing public was introduced to a reflective, kinder, gentler soul. By the time of the inauguration, the transformation was complete. His address was praised for its balanced, thoughtful comment, as well as for its delivery. While a few commented that he could not compete, in style at least, with the "Great Communicator," President Bush presented himself as a thinking man, a man of substance. In the background symbolism flourished while the White House received its new occupants. The Gipper saluted Bush when he and Nancy departed, and the new president saluted back.

Bush inherited many difficult problems. Underpinning all, however, was the enormous task of separating symbolism from illusion, perhaps duplicity. He had to assume responsibility for the visual and verbal rhetoric of the campaign, as well as for the symbols of the previous administration with which he had become so unmistakably identified. Ceremonial images had to be squared with reality. Bush continually implored voters to "Read my lips . . . no more taxes." Many recalled that in 1979 those same lips shaped the words "voodoo economics." Even as the Great Communicator praised the family in his farewell address, he submitted a budget that reduced aid to the homeless by 50%. Inspiring pictures of the Bush family can only magnify the painful images of families that slipped below the poverty level during the past eight years. Pride in the nation will not, by itself, change America's status as a debtor nation, spotted with decayridden cities, a fabulously rich country where at least 20% of the children are poor. Self-confidence in ourselves and in the land exist alongside eight years of disregard for conservation and an increasingly polluted earth. The balance between symbol and substance will not be easy to restore. If this imbalance should not be addressed, the stunning political portraits and patriotic audiovisual hymns to the American way can become empty ideological propaganda.

As Americans have accepted the made-for-TV political icons, they have also conceded the power to define political leadership to media managers who mold and shape the candidates' images for particular

markets. One might expect the press corps to have raised more questions about these issues. ABC Washington reporter Sam Donaldson
summed up the problem when he remarked, "That bunch in the White
House discovered that an image is worth a thousand facts."[9] One might
ask, what has happened to the critical watchdog role that Americans expect the press to play?

Some observers believe that contrary to the clichés about the liberal press, network journalists have tilted toward a very uncritical posture
in their coverage of politics, especially during the Reagan era. In analyzing this faintheartedness, Mark Crispin Miller points out that reporters
generally make an effort not to promote ideology. As professionals, their
sympathies are neither left nor right. But to counteract their personal
convictions, which are often liberal, they lean over backwards to be uncritical of conservatives. Moreover, they serve commercial television networks whose aims are to promote ratings.[10]

In another critique of the press, Mark Hertsgaard details specific
instances of "jelly-bean" journalism during the last eight years. In the
face of explicit media management the press seemed to turn its head or
back away from critical scrutiny, from the 1981 tax breaks, from Star
Wars, from the Iran-Contra scandal. Far from being a watchdog, the
press has become blasé and deferential. Yet the blame for the deteriora-
tion of the critical role of the media, he says, should also be borne by
Reagan and media managers, such as Michael Deaver, who marketed
and sold "official myths," developing sophisticated new models for manipulating public opinion. Packaging of the nation's policies and leader
debased the presidential office, as well as the role of the press in a
democracy. Finally, says Hertsgaard, the public must also assume some
responsibility for allowing themselves to be titillated, or benumbed, by
dazzling visuals and prepackaged stories. Citizens of the United States
have much more freedom to challenge governmental policies than do
persons in most countries. The signs of news manipulation *were* present—the elimination of regular press conferences and the staged emotional appeals to influence public opinions—but the public, like the press
seemed not to see or hear. People and press passively accepted the
agenda set in the White House. A fresh debate on the role of the media
in a democratic society, Hertsgaard maintains, is now essential.[11]

In the public sphere we have celebrated myths of liberty, diversity,
pluralism, and a second chance to achieve the good life. Yet, ironically,
as TV's role in political campaigns increased, voter participation de-

clined. In recent elections as few as 26% of the potential voters may elect a president and Congress, and enact policy. If commercial broadcasting then reinforces and acclaims this decisive minority as truly representative, the TV icons and rituals assume awesome dimensions. It is far from clear how truly representative they are of the millions who have slipped through the cracks in the system.

The purpose of this chapter has been to draw attention to the symbolic worlds we enter when we go beyond the boundaries of everyday routines and try to think about our corporate life. Prior to the information revolution, public symbols that bridged personal and communal experience were located in city squares and cathedrals. Today, access to our abstract, larger world is found in mass media, as we read the newspaper, switch on the radio, turn on the TV. Like medieval peasants who left their fields to gape at pictures in stone and glass authorized by ecclesiastics, we are equally dependent upon institutional images to explain the larger system to which we belong.

As the fine arts of the twentieth century moved deeper into the private visions of individual artists, the power and responsibility for the communication of shared, public meanings have been taken over by the popular arts, especially television. Pervasive print and electronic media have for decades expressed and celebrated the values of a secular society. The technological revolution in image-making sparked a sacramental revolution. Like belief systems of the past, contemporary institutions—political and economic—have come to depend upon images to give concrete expression to tenets of faith and to construct pictures of order and authority. Arts generally considered inferior or commercial now perform functions similar to those of the monumental arts of previous cultures. Like those revered stained-glass windows or carved statuary of earlier times, the elusive representations of TV depict a mythological framework for contemporary individual and collective life.

– 6 –

Power and Pleasure in Video Texts

Robert Scholes

The approach to video that I am proposing here is by way of a theory of rhetoric, a theory that runs counter to the view of rhetoric most familiar to students of modern literature. The view that I propose to counter is sometimes thought to have an ancient pedigree, but is actually the product of Romantic thinkers. We are especially familiar with it because it was restated powerfully by the major figures of modernist literature in the early part of this century. It is deeply indebted, for instance, to the thinking of both William Butler Yeats and James Joyce. In this view rhetoric is located in binary opposition to something called poetry, literature, or art, with rhetoric occupying the negative slot in this highly charged binarism. Joyce, for instance, tells us that proper art leads to contemplation of the aesthetic object, while improper art (or rhetoric) moves us to action rather than contemplation. Yeats says, in a beautifully telling phrase, that he makes rhetoric out of his quarrels with others and poetry out of his quarrels with himself. Such a view positions rhetoric as the study of improper art, the theory and practice of manipulative textuality, as opposed to the pure textuality of art or literature. This view would seem to make rhetoric the perfect way of approaching television, which is widely held to be the least proper and impurest form of text known to humanity. As I have indicated, however, I am arguing against this view for a number of reasons, one of which is that I do not believe that any proper or pure form of textuality exists. As Jacques Derrida might have said, there is no form of textuality outside of rhetoric. Before abandoning it, however, we can learn something from the notion of rhetoric and aesthetics as locked in an invidious opposition.

We should begin, perhaps, by noting that this opposition between rhetoric and aesthetics was developed and deployed by post-Enlightenment thinkers. A. G. Baumgarten is usually credited with introducing the term *aesthetics* (in the sense of the study of "taste") to European discourse in the middle of the eighteenth century. In English the word appears (and is contested) only in the 1830s. The noun *aesthete*, it is worth noting, does not occur in English for another half-century, appearing just in time for James Joyce's birth. The concept of aesthetic activity is connected, historically and logically, with the notion of art and literature as an autonomous area of human life that might be studied under the heading of taste or judgment. In contrast to this, we should remember that Plato and Aristotle position rhetoric in binary opposition not to poetry but to dialectic, the arts of persuasion being opposed to the search for truth. Plato, it is worth remembering, positions most poetry against dialectic as well, so that for him poetry and rhetoric are linked by their lack of concern for truth. For Plato, these oppositions are normally quite invidious: Dialectic is good, rhetoric and poetry are not. Aristotle is much less absolute. For him, rhetoric and dialectic are "counterparts" (see the opening of the *Rhetoric*[1]) that function together in human discourse, meeting in the form of the enthymeme. He also suggests that rhetoric and poetry are closely allied, both being designed to arouse the passions and thus necessarily using many of the same means to accomplish these same ends.

The point of this brief excursion into the history of rhetorical and aesthetic theory is that the medium of television will respond better to an approach that takes its departure from Aristotle than from the modernist heirs of Romanticism. I say Aristotle and not Plato here, for reasons that I trust will be obvious. Plato prefers and seeks purity of form. His dialectic is in fact a method for the purification of thought. Aristotle, on the other hand, is comfortable among the mixed forms of ordinary living. In particular, he tells us early in his treatise on the subject, that rhetoric "has to do with things about which we commonly deliberate—things for which we have no special art or science; and with the sort of hearers who cannot grasp many points in a single view, or follow a long chain of reasoning." This is indeed the very stuff of television and the other mass media as well. We need, then, a rhetoric of video in the Aristotelian sense of rhetoric, looking at the manner in which video texts mingle their ingredients to please and persuade audiences.

This is not the occasion, nor am I the person, to offer anything approaching a full Aristotelian analysis of the aims and devices of video rhetoric. It should be possible, however, to consider a few video texts in the light of Aristotelian principles and in the spirit of Aristotelian investigation. Aristotle, you will remember, recognized three types of persuasion: that based on the character of the speaker, that based on controlling the emotion of the audience, and that based upon reasoning or argument. Of these, the second is most important for the analysis of video, I should think, though it is by no means the only type we find in video texts. In this essay, however, we shall concentrate upon this second type, of which Aristotle says that it obtains power over the audience by emotional means. This type of persuasion can be thought of in terms of what I should like to call "textual economy", that is to say, of some exchange of values for which texts are the medium.

Textual economy is marked, in particular, by exchanging images of power and pleasure. The rhetoric of textual economy that I am proposing, then, will take the form of an investigation into the flow of pleasure and power that is organized by any text. Both texts and other forms of human intercourse may be described as systems in which power and pleasure are exchanged. For instance, there is a profound analogy between textual and sexual exchanges, an analogy of which T. S. Eliot (to name a modernist with a more developed theory of rhetoric than Yeats or Joyce) was fully aware. Eliot put textual matters in terms of an eroto-political metaphor that may help us get our bearings here. In a letter he wrote to Stephen Spender in 1935, Eliot described our reading of literary texts in the following words: "You don't really criticize any author to whom you have never surrendered yourself. . . . Even just the bewildering minute counts: you have to give yourself up, and then recover yourself, and the third moment is having something to say, before you have wholly forgotten both surrender and recovery." Frank Kermode, whose discussion of this passage provides the point of departure for me here,[2] notes that the expression "bewildering minute," which Eliot had used in two of his important essays in addition to this letter to Spender, is taken from a passage in a Jacobean play by Tourneur or Middleton:

Are lordships sold to maintain ladyships
For the benefit of a bewildering minute?

As Kermode points out, in their context the lines refer quite un-
ambiguously to the erotic experience of "sexual surrender," and he per-
spicuously traces Eliot's transformation of them in *The Waste Land*
("blood shaking my heart/The awful daring of a moment's surrender")
and other poems and essays, where they are used to signify both sexual
and spiritual surrenders. What Eliot and Kermode both seem to overlook or suppress—in what we can now see as a typically modernist critical gesture—is the word "sold" in the original Jacobean quotation. The
"bewildering minute" of pleasure is positioned by the playwright within
a politico-economic system in which lordships may be exchanged for
sexual pleasure. My rhetorical point here is simply that textual pleasure
also always involves some surrender of sovereignty, and that this is true
whether the text is a poem or a TV advertisement. *The Waste Land* itself
is designed to persuade us of the degradation (or abjection, as Calvin
Bedient would have it) of a life without religious commitment, and we
cannot "surrender" to the pleasure of Eliot's text without at least trying
on his beliefs during that bewildering moment of surrender. *The Waste
Land*, then, is rhetorical in just the sense that I am proposing for that
term. What it does, in its own way, and for its own audience, is exactly
what video texts, including commercials, do for their audiences. The differences are only in the constraints and opportunities offered by the different media. The economy of power and pleasure is the same. And
they begin with the bewildering minute (or, in the case of television commercials, the bewildering few seconds).

The moments of surrender proposed to us by video texts come in
many forms, but all involve a complex dynamic of power and pleasure.
We are, for instance, offered a kind of power through the enhancement
of our vision. Close-ups position us where we could never stand. Slow
motion allows us an extraordinary penetration into the mechanics of
movement, and, combined with music, lends a balletic grace to ordinary
forms of locomotion. Filters and other devices cause us to see the world
through jaundiced or rose-colored optics, coloring events with emotion
more effectively and less obtrusively than verbal pathetic fallacy. These
derangements of normal visual processing can be seen as either constraints or extensions of visual power—as power over the viewer or as extensions of the viewer's own optical power—or both. Either way, they

offer us what is perhaps the greatest single virtue of art: change from the normal, a defense against the ever-present threat of boredom. Video texts, like all except the most utilitarian forms of textuality, are constructed upon a base of boredom from which they promise us relief.

Visual fascination (and I have only mentioned a few of its obvious forms) is just one of the matrices of power and pleasure that are organized by video texts. Others include narrativity and what I should like to call, at least tentatively, cultural reinforcement. By narrativity, of course, I mean the pleasures and powers associated with the reception of stories presented in video texts. By cultural reinforcement, I mean the process through which video texts confirm viewers in their ideological positions and reassure them of their membership in a collective cultural body. This function, which is at once religious and political, is an extremely important element of video textuality, and indeed, an extremely important dimension of all the mass media. This is a function performed throughout much of human history by literature and the other arts, but now, as the arts have become more estranged from their own culture and even opposed to it, the mass media have come to perform this role. What the epic poem did for ancient cultures, the romance for feudalism, and the novel for bourgeois society, the media, and especially television, now do for the commodified, bureaucratized world that is our present environment.

It is time, now, to see how these processes operate in some specific video texts; for example, the well-known Budweiser "Black Umpire" commercial. In this video text, which runs for thirty seconds, we are given enough information to construct an entire life story—provided we have the cultural knowledge upon which this construction depends. The story we construct is that of a young man from the provinces, in this case a black man pursuing a career as a baseball umpire, who gets his "big break," his chance to make it in the big city, to rise to the top of his profession. We see him working hard in the small-time, small-town atmosphere of the minor leagues, where the pace of events is slower and more relaxed than it is "at the top." Then he gets his chance for success, and we see him as he passes his first real test successfully. He must call an important and "close" play correctly, and then withstand the pressure of dispute, neither giving ground by changing his mind (which would be fatal) nor reacting too vigorously to the challenge of his call by an offended manager. His passing of this test and being accepted is indicated by the scene in the bar, in which the manager toasts the umpire with a bottle of Budweiser beer. From this scene we conclude that the ump has now "made it," and will live happily ever after.

From a few brief scenes, then, and aided by the voice-over narration, we construct an entire life. How do we do this? We draw upon a repertory of cultural information that extends from fairy tales and other basic narrative structures to knowledge about the game and business of baseball. As a way of making more concrete the importance of cultural knowledge, it is worth watching this commercial imagining that you are from some part of the world where baseball is scarcely known. Suppress your knowledge of baseball, both the game and its corporate structure, and suppose, for instance, that you are an Austrian woman studying to be a physician.

Try it sometime and you will see that such an exercise is very difficult. Nevertheless, in so doing we are reminded that in processing a narrative text we actually construct the story by bringing a vast repertory of cultural knowledge to bear upon the text that we are contemplating. Our pleasure in the narrative is to some extent a constructive pleasure, based upon the sense of accomplishment we achieve by successfully completing this task. By "getting" the story, we prove our competence and demonstrate our membership in a cultural community. And what, in the case of the Budweiser commercial, is the story that we "get"? It is the myth of America itself, of the racial melting pot, of upward mobility, of justice done without fear or favor. The corporate structure of baseball, with minor leagues offering a path for the talented to the celebrity and financial rewards of the majors, embodies values that we all possess, we Americans, as one of the deepest parts of our cultural heritage or ideology. It is, of course, on the playing field that talent triumphs most easily over racial or social barriers. Every year in baseball new faces arrive. Young men, having proved themselves in the minors, get their chance to perform at the highest level. Princeton graduates and high school dropouts who speak little or no English are judged equally by how well they hit, run, throw, and react to game situations. If baseball is still "the national pastime," it is because in it our cherished myths materialize, or appear at least to materialize.

This particular commercial is especially interesting because it shows us a black man competing not with his body but with his mind, his judgment, and his emotions, in a cruelly testing public arena. Americans who attend to sports are aware that black athletes are just beginning to find acceptance at certain "leadership" positions, such as quarterback in professional football, and that there is still an active scandal over the slender representation of blacks at baseball's managerial and corporate levels. The case of the black umpire reminds viewers of these problems, even as it suggests that here, too, talent will finally prevail. The system works. America works. We can take pride in this. The narrative reduces its story to the absolutely bare essentials; making a career turn, or seem to turn, rests on a close decision. The ump must make a close call, which will be fiercely contested by a manager who is deliberately testing him. This is a story of initiation, in that respect, an ordeal that the ump must meet successfully. The text ensures that we know this is a text, by showing us the manager plotting in his dugout, and it gives us a manager with one of those baseball faces (Irish? German?) that have the history of the game written on them. This is not just partisan versus impartial judge, it is old man against youth, and white against black. We root for the umpire because we want the system to work, not just baseball but the whole thing: America. For the story to work, of course, the ump must make the right call, and we must know it to be right. Here, the close-up and slow motion come into play—just as they would in a real instant replay—to let us see both how close the call is and that the umpire has indeed made the right call. The runner is out. The manager's charge from the dugout is classic baseball protest, and the ump's self-control and slow walk away from the angry manager are gestures in a ritual we all know. That's right, we think, that's the way it's done. We know these moves the way the contemporaries of Aeschylus and Sophocles knew the myths upon which the Greek tragedies were based. Baseball is already a ritual, and a ritual we partake of mostly through the medium of television. The commercial has only to organize these images in a certain way to create a powerful narrative.

At the bar after the game, we are offstage, outside that ritual of baseball, but we are still in the world of myth. The manager salutes the ump with his tilted bottle of Bud: The old man acknowledges that youth has passed its test. The sword on the shoulder of knighthood, the laying-on of hands, the tilted Bud—all these are ritual gestures in the same narrative structure of initiation. To the extent that we have wanted this to happen we are gratified by this closing scene of the narrative text, and many things, as I have suggested, conspire to make us want this ending. We are dealing with an archetypal narrative that has been adjusted for maximum effect within a particular political and social context, and all this has been deployed with a technical skill in casting, directing, acting, photographing, and editing that is of a high order. It is very hard to resist the pleasure of this text and we cannot accept the pleasure without, for the bewildering minute at least, also accepting the ideology that is so rich and closely entangled with the story that we construct from the video text. To accept the pleasure of this text is to believe that America works. This is a comforting belief, itself a pleasure of an even higher order, as long as we can maintain it. Does the text also sell Budweiser? This is something only market research (if you believe it) can tell. But it surely sells the American way first and then seeks to sell its brand of beer by establishing a metonymic connection between the product and the nation: a national beer for the national pastime.

An audience that can understand this commercial, successfully constructing the ump's story from the scenes represented in the text and the comments of the narrative voice, is an audience that understands narrative structure and has a significant amount of cultural knowledge as well, including both data (how baseball leagues are organized, for instance, and how the game is played) and myth (what constitutes "success," for example, and what "initiation" is). At a time when certain critics, such as William Bennett and E. D. Hirsch, are bewailing our ignorance of culture, it is important to realize that Americans are not without culture; many Americans simply have a different culture from that of Bennett and Hirsch. What they really lack, for the most part, is any way of analyzing and criticizing the power of a text like this Budweiser commercial: not its power to sell beer, which is easily resisted, especially once you have tasted better beer, but its power to sell America. For the sort of analysis that I am suggesting, it is necessary to recover (as Eliot says) from the surrender to this text, and it is also necessary to have the tools of ideological criticism. Recovery, in fact, may depend upon critical analysis, which is why the analysis of video texts needs to be taught in all our schools.

Before moving on to the consideration of a more complex textual economy, we would do well to pause and consider the necessity of ideological criticism. One dimension of the conservative agenda for this country has been conspicuously anticritical. The proposals of William Bennett and E. D. Hirsch, for instance, different as they are in certain respects, are both recipes for the indoctrination of young people in certain cultural myths. The Great Books of past ages, in the eyes of Bennett, Hirsch, and Allan Bloom, are to be mythologized, turned into frozen monuments of greatness in which our "cultural heritage" is embodied. This is precisely what Bloom does to Plato, for instance, turning the dialectical search for truth into a fixed recipe for "greatness of soul." The irony of this is that Plato can only die in the process. Plato's work can be kept alive in our time only by such irreverent critiques as that of Jacques Derrida, who takes Plato seriously as an opponent, which is to say, takes him dialectically. In this age of massive manipulation and disinformation, criticism is the only way we have of taking something seriously. The greatest patriots of our time will be those who explore our ideology critically, with particular attention to the gaps between mythology and practice. Above all, we must start with our most beloved icons, not the ones we profess allegiance to, but those that really have the power to move and shake us. I propose to conclude this discussion by examining such an icon, as it existed for my own generation, across the media of film, radio, phonograph, and television. More current icons I shall prudently leave to more current investigators. Each generation has its own work to do. The video text with which I am here concerned is the famous "Somewhere Over the Rainbow" concert of Judy Garland in tramp costume. The first time I saw this video, which, as it happens, was not so very long ago, I found myself experiencing an extraordinarily bewildering minute, moved more deeply—and, as it turns out, further—than I could readily account for. My "recovery" from this event, to use Eliot's term, was effected through a process of critical analysis that is now embodied in this text. I present it here in hopes that my own experience is sufficiently typical to be of some worth as an example, while also hoping, of course, that my critical analysis will be sufficiently developed to transcend that typical experience—to be, in fact, critical. I shall begin by offering a description of the video text itself.

From its opening moment, this text is not a single or simple entity, in time, space, or emotional register. The first voice we hear is that of Liza Minelli, telling us that we are about to watch a rare recording of her mother Judy Garland (who is now, of course, long dead) singing in concert the song through which she first became an icon to the American public. We then see Judy Garland, dressed in the tramp costume that she used in the previous number of her routine. She comes downstage to sit close to the audience, and the camera moves in to meet her. As she sings the song, she begins to weep, at times appearing barely able to continue singing, and her voice, always highly emotional, seems on certain notes almost to cry of pain. The tramp makeup, with its heavily blackened and smudged face, gives Garland the appearance of a street urchin at times, while at other moments she shows her age. The image becomes, for the knowledgeable viewer, a tissue of distinct but related times: our own viewing time, the time of Minelli's narration, which is after her mother's death, the time of the recording, with its distance from us and its authenticity signified by the black-and-white photography itself, and all the other times we have seen or heard Judy Garland sing this song, especially the first time we saw her singing it for the first time (first time for us and first time for her) in the film *The Wizard of Oz*. We as viewers are aware of this collection of moments though how consciously may vary from one person to another. These separate moments catch up in their net the time that has passed between one and another. We are aware, then, at some level, of the difference between ourselves as we were when we first saw Judy Garland singing this song, and, as we are now. Because she has existed as a celebrity in this culture, we are aware of the story of her life as it has entered our cultural awareness, becoming a mythic narrative of the unhappiness of the successful: a story of debauchery and dissolution. Many of us, viewers of her own generation, will remember images of her from other films, seeing her, for instance, as the bloated and faded image of defeated Germany in *Judgment at Nuremberg*, and having seen, in that image, her own life's defeat and dissolution, the abuse of alcohol and barbiturates that, our cultural mythology tells us, led to her early death.

This past, I am arguing, weighs upon us as we watch her singing this song, and it is a double past: her life, as we know it from the popular media, and our own lives, as we have constructed them in our own video of memory. It is because we cannot see her now, without remembering her then, that we cannot escape remembering ourselves then at the moment of our present viewing. This video icon, by its inexorable emotional and temporal logic, forces us to take account of the years between its two major moments. We are thus led to be aware of our lives as lived in time. Beyond this, we become aware of the difference between the way we are now and the way that we thought then that we might be now. Our former hopes and dreams are evoked by this video text, as we ineluctably make narrative the material presented to us. Given so many spots of time, we have no choice but to connect them in two parallel narratives, hers and ours. All this is, of course, enhanced by the subject matter of the song, though the song expresses the same distances through metaphors of space rather than time: the difference between being here and that other place, over the rainbow; the difference, as the film textualizes it, between Kansas and Oz.

In the film *The Wizard of Oz*, Dorothy sings this song early, while she is still in Kansas, and she sings it without tears. The film positions the song as a childish wish for a richer, fuller life, a utopian vision which the cinematic narrative betrays by treating the whole trip to Oz as the product of a delirious dream brought on by the concussion that Dorothy sustains during the cyclone. The film, in marked contrast to the novel upon which it was based, rationalizes the fantastic and uses it to force Dorothy to accept the reality principle. Oz, not history, becomes the nightmare from which Dorothy needs to escape. Given this, it is interesting that Judy Garland's public has always interpreted her life as the story of a girl for whom reality was not enough, as the description of her funeral by Mel Tormé illustrates:

> There were no hysterically shrieking women [as there were at Valentino's funeral], but many people in the long queue wept unashamedly as they filed past the girl-woman lying in state inside Campbell's. On leaving the parlor, one middle-aged lady dabbed at tear-streaked cheeks with a piece of Kleenex and intoned, "Well, she's found that rainbow now."[3]

People living lives well this side of the rainbow, who would not trade them for the disaster that was Judy Garland's life, nevertheless found in that life an admirable myth of rejection, of refusal to accept what we all accept in the way of life in this country at this time. It is this myth, already present in the consciousness of certain viewers, that becomes the source of power for the video image of Judy, the girl-woman, singing this song about an alternative universe about which we learn no single physical detail.

It is worth noting, if only in passing, that Dorothy's song is, in its sentiments, strikingly close to a more complex piece of music, sung by another trapped young woman, in another country:

> Stridono lassù,
> liberamente lanciati a vol,
> a vol come frecci, gli augel.
> Disfidani le nubi e'l sol cocente,
> e vanno, e vanno per le vie del ciel. . . .
> Vanno laggiù, verso un paese strano
> che sognan forse e che cercano invan.

They cry out up above,
freely launched in flight,
flying like arrows, the birds.
They challenge the clouds and the blazing sun,
and they travel along the roads of the sky. . . .
They travel far off, toward a strange land
that perhaps they dream and seek in vain.

These are lines from Nedda's song, in Act I of I Pagliacci, as she dreams of escaping from her oppressively jealous husband, and they should remind us here, especially if we can remember the haunting melody that goes with them, that the emotion they arouse in the viewer is rooted in the life and situation of the fictional character, while the emotion generated by Judy Garland singing "Over the Rainbow" on stage is generated by the fiction of her life. Both of these fictions, we should remember, are the creations of the viewers, though grounded in different texts.

The opera is relevant here in many ways because it is an opera about the mixture of life and theater, with an audience onstage applauding the realism of acting generated by a clown who is genuinely bent upon murdering his wife. Judy Garland, we should remember, liked to perform "Over the Rainbow" still wearing the clownish tramp's costume she used for the preceding song. I am suggesting that the interpenetration of art and life upon which the effect of this song depends is not gratuitous but part of the act that Garland developed, an act that included her life. Just as in the opera Nedda's husband Canio must laugh while his heart is breaking, Judy Garland must sometimes have wept while her heart jumped for joy. What her audience took to be life breaking in upon art, the real penetrating into the unreal, was in fact itself part of the rhetoric of her performance—which is not, however, to say that such rhetoric is invented ex nihilo. The life that she is using, textualized by film magazines and scandal sheets, is nevertheless a life she lived. Not only is there no perfect separation between rhetoric and art, there is none between life as textualized and life as lived, either. This perverse thesis (as you may find it) is born out of Mel Tormé's account of seeing Garland perform the song at the Palace Theatre in 1951. He saw her once and went backstage to congratulate her. When he said he wanted to come a second time she tried to discourage him. Here (in abridged form) is his account of both visits:

1. The moment Garland stepped onto the stage and proceeded to dazzle the packed house with "Swanee," "Rock-a-Bye Your Baby" "San Francisco," and the myriad other Garland classics, I finally knew what everyone had been shouting about. And the final pin-dropping moments when she sat, in the tramp costume on the edge of the stage, legs dangling over, lighted only by a single spotlight, and sang "Over the Rainbow" was for me, and everyone else, one of the few really great pieces of theater we would ever see.

2. Two weeks later I returned to the Palace. The reception and attendant ovation for her was, if anything, greater than on the previous occasion. But I saw what she meant [in urging him not to see it again]. I wasn't really disappointed, but having reacted to the first performance on a purely sensory basis, I was now inured enough to examine her act technically. When she sang "Over the Rainbow," the tears rolled down her cheeks at the precise moment they had flowed the last time I had seen her. Later, in her dressing room, she said, "You were surprised when I cried 'on cue' in 'Rainbow,' weren't you? Now admit it, bub, you were surprised and disappointed."

"Like hell I was," I countered. "It just reaffirmed what I already knew: you're not only one hell of a singer, you're a tremendous actress."

"I know," she added, without a drop of conceit, merely acknowledging a proven fact. "But sometimes when I turn the tears on, people who have seen me here before go away disappointed."[4]

Mel Tormé experienced the bewildering moment of surrender, and only recovered on his second viewing. At that point he could become critical, but only in a "technical" way, as one actor to another. He does not raise the question of what we exchange for our emotional pleasure in this performance. For him the emotional effect is an end in itself. But we must raise this question and shall return to it, after attending to one or two other matters. Not everyone, of course, responds to the Budweiser commercial or to Judy Garland in the manner that I have indicated. I showed these video texts to some visitors from Germany, and found that they could scarcely follow the outline of the story of the black umpire and did not really know what had happened. Certainly, they did not feel any surge of American patriotism in watching that little tale. Nor were they moved by Judy Garland. One of them thought Garland seemed to be having lung trouble, not even recognizing that the famous tears were supposed to be signs of sorrow or suffering. They found the emotion absurd and forced, to the extent that they noticed that it was present at all. They were, in fact, scarcely engaged by either of the two video texts that they looked at for me, because they could bring to neither the cultural information that was required to complete the texts in a fashion commensurate with the words, images, and music presented.

Part of my point here is that both texts engage only those readers who share the requisite cultural information. Another part is that these two apparently different texts, one clearly "advertising" and the other just as clearly "art" or "entertainment," are both thoroughly rhetorical in that they are sites where pleasure and power are interchanged. In the case of the Budweiser commercial, we noted that we exchange our pleasure in that narrative for a share of the American dream, for a cultural reinforcement that is also pleasurable. What we give up, at least until we recover, is the ability to take an imaginative stand outside that dream and to criticize it. This we can accomplish only by the active labor of thought, comparing the textual narrative with information from other sources, including our own experience. Such an achievement of critical thought carries its own power and pleasure, of course, but we obtain these only by consciously putting aside the pleasure of the text and its attendant narrative.

In the case of the Garland video, the process is similar. We read the performance of "Over the Rainbow" as a scene in a double narrative, the story of Judy Garland's life and that of our own. We are pleased by her tears because they are authenticated by the myth of the unhappy and doomed celebrity, which makes our own failures and frustrations pale in comparison. As we watch her, we think that she is in so much mental anguish that she can barely sing, she almost fails to entertain at all. Her failures clothe her and give a kind of authentication to her tramp's attire and makeup: an authentication that is at once spurious and ultimate. On the one hand, she is acting. She does this on cue, performance after performance. On the other hand, we have her life story, ending in the ultimate authentication, her messy, quasi-suicidal death. We scarcely need Theodor Adorno to remind us that she has packaged her life in order to present it to us as the ultimate commodity in a world that reifies and commodifies everything. This, too, is a rhetoric, but whether it is the ultimate betrayal of art or a mode of art as authentic as any other in this culture is impossible, for me, at least, to say. To "recover" from the power of this rhetoric is, on the one hand, as easy as the method of Mel Tormé—we need only see a second performance—and, on the other, as hard as imagining the authenticity that may lie on the other side of the rhetorical rainbow itself.

– 7 –

In Video Veritas:
The Mythic Structures of Video Dynamics

E. David Thorp

Post-Text

In 1513 and 1514, Albrecht Dürer (1471-1528), in his early for-ties, created three masterly engravings (in this context, let us think of them as icons) that particularly illuminated his own uncertainties over values in visual art and, in our case, video art.[1] In the first, "Knight, Death, and the Devil," a knight rides through a craggy landscape, his dog running beside him, while a rotted and crowned Satan and a boar-faced, harrow-carrying Death stand ineffectually beside the road. In the second, "Saint Jerome in his Study," St. Jerome sits at work, his dog and his lion resting on the floor in front of him. In the third, "Melencolia I," a winged woman sits next to an unfinished monument or building. Beside her a winged boy sits perched on a column capital and a sheep sleeps at her feet.

All three are documents of Dürer's quest for precedents, icons, and values, as it were, requiring interpretation, demanding from the viewer something more than seeing. In each we see a central figure: a sixteenth-century knight and saint in the first two, and in the third an apparition of our contemporary video artist engaged in a vocation, a way of life. The difference lies in the assurance and the direction of the last way.

The knight moves through a rough world, not unlike our own, but is scarcely bothered by the threats along the way. In fact, Dürer depicts both the Devil and Death as somewhat comical figures, as if the engraving, his icon, were done by the knight for whom they were only empty costumes meant to scare children. Saint Jerome, on the other hand, is bent over his task of writing. Around him the world is ordered, comfortable, and complete; and the normally assertive and kingly lion is as placid and domesticated as a lapdog. Like the knight, Jerome has a clear sense of where his work is going and he commits himself to it wholeheartedly.

Melencolia, however, our twentieth-century video artist unaccountably placed in the sixteenth century, is quite upset. Around her are the implements of measure, tools, and building blocks. In our mind's eye, her measure is a 3-minute music television tape; her tool is a 28-second mass media advertisement; and her building block is a 45-minute "video icons and values" formal conference presentation. But whether she is in the middle of a project or just beginning, either she doesn't know what to do with them or what she can do is insufficient for her aspiration. In twentieth-century psychological terms, she is blocked. All the practical means are at hand, but without the shaping vision, they are useless.[2]

Just as the knight and the saint can be understood as models for values in a mood of assurance, Melencolia is an emblem of uncertainty: uncertainty about both the artistic calling and what that calling implies in actual work. The knight and the saint are self-contained and self-willed, perhaps because they have missions outside themselves, whether chivalric or religious. Melencolia, however, lacks that inner certainty of mission. Independent of any master, she doesn't know how to become the master of herself. The romantic knight and the literary saint have clear and compelling missions. But what is the mission of the video artist? Is she all assertion and no subject matter?

Unlike the other two iconic engravings, one set on the road and the other in a room, "Melencolia I" is cluttered with objects and depicts an essentially unrealistic space.[3] Unlike the "Knight, Death and the Devil," and "Saint Jerome in his Study," "Melencolia" is a work that exists totally in the mind. Here Dürer most directly dramatizes his fears about his artistic vocation, but he also requires the viewer to match his own intelligence to the demands of the engraving. Its clear paradox is that, while artists especially may suffer the tortures of despair about their skills and their understanding, their depiction of that struggle can become subject matter itself. Dürer may have been the first artist to turn melancholy into a special attribute of artists. But by the end of the sixteenth century, every young man or woman who wanted to be thought sensitive was wearing the melancholic look and dressing in whatever the melancholic style demanded. By the end of the twentieth century, will it be said that every young person who wants to be thought sensitive will be carrying about the equivalent of today's Sony, Panasonic, Hitachi, or JVC video production systems to develop images by which inner life might be known more directly?

Five hundred years later, shall we give a new title to Dürer's "Melencolia I" as her writing block becomes our building block: "In Video Veritas: The Mythic Structures of Video Dynamics"? Mythically, can we look again with Dürer for the structural assurances of the knight and the saint? Dynamically, can we experience with Dürer's insight the Melencolia as freshly as her image was born 474 years ago?

Ah, Melencolia! In the formal, academic setting, how vague if not lax become our attempts at defining the video artist.[4] Her field is so vast, including genres of tapes, music videos, museum installations, and general mass media productions. Yes, there is interdisciplinary respectability. Video art motivates close exchanges between sociology, semiotics, and psychoanalysis. Columns of texts at first glance promise a healthy methodological hybridization. But a closer look all too often reveals *pre texts* (user group oral communications), *texts* (publications of proceedings), and *post texts* (iconostasis of proceedings) with themes developing not in a continuous or progressive way but by a series of jumps, echoes, combinations, disagreements, and reversals. Now we know why it is that a winged boy sits perched on a column capital next to Melencolia in Dürer's engraving: This youth is more readily adaptable to new technologies than to theories long cultural traditions represent. More often mythical than real, he flies from the top of iconic discourses the moment his own incompleteness is attacked. Of equal value to music and live dance and possibly someday to a live liturgy, this Ganymede to Melencolia cannot be imprisoned on a pedestal. Chains of association are more stimulating for him than exact descriptions, inner images more appropriate to his flight path than other kinds of interpretations. An absence of a specific video language is not felt by him as a real lack. His break with traditional perceptions through experiments that conflict with traditional processes governing our experience of verbal times and spaces is his reason for being. His wings or image and sound—videorythmics—form a living body, possibly as immortal as they are puzzling.

At the end of this essay, I will pre-textually expand upon this love affair between Ganymede and Melencolia. By way of a melancholic dress rehearsal, however, let us now explore current levels of attraction and/or estrangement between Ganymede and the romantic knight laughing at Death and the Devil, and between Ganymede and the saintly Jerome in his literary study.

Text

How are we to play the role of Ganymede to the knight laughing at Death and the Devil? And where has he flown to, away from his perch atop the textual column unfinished by Melencolia? He is now at the Global Village Video Center affiliated with the New School for Social Research in Manhattan. The clock on the wall indicates broadcast time.

High-spirited students have scarcely any time at all for writing papers other than scripting as they perform various functions on a rotating basis: multiple camera operations, sound recording and mixing, special effects generating, lighting, technical directing. Electronic video and computer editing skills are honed to perfection for documentary, music, and investigative reporting projects. "To the devil with video theory and a Ph.D.!" After six to twelve months of study, the FCC license for employment with ABC, CBS, and NBC uptown (if not the Juilliard School of Music or Lincoln Center) requires the mastery of dozens of texts on such subjects as theory of modulation, FM and AM spectrum allocation charts, basic circuit analysis, solid state theory, microwave and receiver theory, circuitry and attendant theory, trouble-shooting and diagnosis of video equipment, including both industrial and processional broadcast grades, FCC rules and regulations, current broadcast standards and broadcast station operations, and a pragmatic review of FCC test materials. So much for non-graduate school certification!

A portfolio tape for the resumé of a video artist identifies primary project objectives realized with major field production components. Elements of production stressed include selection and preparation of suitable subject matter, use of 3-tube color broadcast camera, portable audio and lighting techniques, production schedules and management, budgeting and funding. Personal styles are developed through video editing, preparation of montage sequences from assigned footage, assignment and editing of an actual news story, documenting rock bands with previously prepared studio mixes involving special effects applications and lip-sync recordings. Working on half-million dollar on-line systems used for videotape mastering, students learn powerful effects available by taking creative works through the rough-cut and final-cut stages on multideck facilities. Character generators driven by a word processor and basic audio processing are used to create professional finished works using efficient state-of-the-art techniques. Interfaces among the computer, time-base correctors, broadcast switcher, and special effects generator provide a broad spectrum for creative choices for both industry-oriented students and artists. Animation, generating and manipulating live video and television signals, creating real-time paintbox and color effects, making use of digitalized equipment for frame squeezing and manipulation are all immeasurably valuable techniques for the production of video icons, images, and symbols.

But what about cultural values? What does Ganymede provide our knight as immunity to a rotted and crowned Satan boring his audience to death? I've discovered that our video artist Melencolia is, indeed, seated amidst the Global Village faculty, sadly set apart from her students. There just isn't time in a broadcast studio to collate her unfinished texts from Japan, the United States, Canada, and from half a dozen leading European contexts, viz., Britain, France, Germany, Belgium, Switzerland, and Yugoslavia. Undermining structural assurances enjoyed by sets, script authors, studio shooting, stock shots in the field, are words and sounds with high-tech abstraction, fragmentation, and superimposition in an interrogation of different electronic treatment of images of the inner life. How are myths made to serve as reflections on images and images made to serve as reflection on myths? Out of the Global Village Video Center is yet to come a video-literary work addressing magnetic technology and its poetry.

Work of this kind in embryological form does exist.[5] Ambitious television has improved its status as art. Allan Bloom and E. D. Hirsh despair of children scared out of their wits by news television or seduced out of their virtues by music television or bored out of their minds by soap operas. The self and its immediate communications environment require a site of more complex performances and investigations.

In Canada, one thinks immediately of the phenomenally successful Trinity Square Video in the basement of Toronto's Holy Trinity
Church: a community-access video facility with lively programs of poetry
readings, performance arts, theater workshops, electronic music, video
and sound works. Questions of reality and identity are rapt externaliza-
tions of the environment of the intimate. Behind the scenes of a media
culture doting on life-styles of the privileged, narcissism, glamour, and
fashion tear sheets come to vacuous life. There is coverage of news
events in which the interests of women are foregrounded, and presentations of the rigorously conceptual work of local artists. For example, a
tape was broadcast employing elements of personal narrative, fictional
reenactment, and collaborative research to produce an empowering analysis of and rebuttal to ways in which women are socialized toward de-
fenselessness. Conventional high-tech documentary is pushed forward to
formal narrative experimentation. If this is a form of *video vérité* drama
that glides along the edge of reality, surrendering intermittently to its
own surreal slipstream, it also announces a new generation of sharp and
energetic vision. Such a dramatization of individuals entrapped within
social forces brings to light a narrative of innocence and jadedness
within moving surfaces of identity. One can ironically employ mystery,
fable, soap opera and other formats of the storyteller's art to render
metaphorically unsettling displacements and startling discoveries within
a shifting base of truths. At the risk of harrowing repetition, Canada
says to us again: Allow the individual woman, if you please, to slip imagination into the ambient space foreign both to the body of the camera
(virtual reality) and to that of the operator (mimetic reality). Prophecy as
poetry, rather than a symbiosis between a computer science-digitalized
photography or the statistical packaging of the social sciences.

In France, Ganymede can help our knight take note of French
video theater shows, especially those in the basement at the Pompidou
Center. The shows offer simultaneous use of video and the performer's
body: Cameras held by multimedia performers or skilled observers play
just as important a role as the scripted bodies. What inner images come
to light? A picture of the body both stylized and realistic, both fixed and
mobile, ingeniously handling illusion, danger, force, fragility, jokes.
There is an ebb and flow of images and sounds with luminescent
graphic elements from one screen to another, searching for an image
perceived and then lost. Thousands of figures and thousands of move-
ments can be technically composed. The switcher inserts, cuts, acceler-

ates and slows images; the computer perfectly edits. As spectators participate in dramatic processes, even technical operations sometimes prove
self-revelatory. Urban rituals with hectic rhythms and obsessive myths:
Are they effects or causes of tape cuttings, inversion of values, color per-
mutations, mixing of synthetic images?

The promise of the Pompidou program: Given a concentration of
technical equipment and the energetic potentials it represents, video may
become the condenser or catalyst of concrete attitudes and behaviors, a
certain way of looking at things that stems from genuine historical and
cultural concerns.

For centuries the Louvre's gallery circles of paintings, models, and
techniques of representation have demanded admiration, but how profoundly they are challenged by having performer/models in video theater authorized to intervene on behalf of their own images. The conceptual prejudice that a person is one and permanent in his or her
anthropometric identity dissolves. Video images comprise a perspective
in anamorphosis, in which memory in its coming and going is made
and unmade simultaneously, forgetful in its trajectory because fearless of
its gravity. With inner images of innocence at high-tech levels, interces-
sions of art can weigh at least as much as the interventions of science.[6]
Accordingly, in his engraving Dürer has placed a sheep safely asleep at
the feet of a good shepherdess, Melencolia. Asleep, because our eyes can
no longer see the truisms of the show or life that have been hidden by
their banality and conformity to a theater or cinema but not a video-gen-
erative model.

From the downstream to the upstream of creation, the video artist
challenges all the conventions that govern the conception, production,
direction, distribution, reception, and consumption of a cultural object.
The end result can be an electronic and poetic gesture or moment or
project that commits the whole being, consequently demanding of the
being to commit itself only in lucid knowledge of the entire process of
the operation or ritual performed or considered. Hence the curriculum
at the Global Village is unfinished until the operations research of the
video engineer approximates the conceptual and cultural grace of a
Museum of Modern Art or a Metropolitan Museum retrospective on
French painters, for example.

Finally, in Japan, Ganymede introduces our knight to the high-
tech wiring of an entire nation by an International Cable Network, a
Value Added Network, and an Information Network System. How un-

finished are our ABC, CBS, and NBC; how insufficient in aspiration!

In Japan, amateur video is already technically accepted as a style. There are groups of home-video makers who supply on a regular basis unedited news material gathered in and around the community to local television stations. Air time is also given to experimental punk video, revealing that video stripped to zero of meaning is a surprisingly tactile, sensual, and expressive medium. Using frame-by-frame editing, one can be inside and outside of the bullet train at the same time. This technique affords a fusion of positive/negative images on the retina of the viewer: images of day and night, beautiful and ugly, good and bad. Notions of old and new are liberated from linear time development. Even mass culture and consumerism float free in this interchangeable video time and space.

Most unique to Japan is the notion of television as the *bonsai* of reality. Real-time video, comparable to traditional Japanese single-stroke painting or single-chisel sculpture, continues to be a favored style of Japanese video makers. At video festivals promoted by hardware manufacturers, the relationship that young artists immersed in a high-tech hybrid environment have to nature is not pacific, but intense and dynamic. Get the best out of nature, they counsel, enjoy intimate relationships of coexistence through technology. Learn, appreciate, master the intricacy of nature's systems. Your tree might turn out to be a mediocre, dwarfed tree or it may turn into a genuine landscape, transcending largeness and smallness, material and mind: nature and ego becoming one. Japan says to us: We must have visions of our own state of being and invite television by way of video to us and not vice versa.[7]

Dürer's knight as video journeyman is, then, a cocky one.[8] He is unafraid of Death and the Devil, not surprised by the rise of a new dilettante who with his zest blows away the lame professional. As we come to value our contemporary video icons, let us wonder at the propensity of established culture to be pushed into a corner while greater innovations, gripping achievements, occur in what has been up to now an entertainment world. What is entertainment but the playful use of image/language relationships for purposes of posing riddles at art and life?

Roland Barthes on myth suggests a way in which practical means for Dürer's Melencolia are at hand. "Myth does not deny things . . . simply, it purifies them, it makes them innocent. In passing from history to nature, myth acts economically; it abolishes the complexity of human acts, it gives them the simplicity of essence. It establishes a bliss-ful clarity: things appear to mean something by themselves."[9] It is said that ours is an age of cultural pessimism and technological optimism and that artists conquer their pessimism by decking themselves out in powerful and positivist technologies. I submit, whatever their fashion-able outerwear may appear to be, it is Roland Barthes, not Calvin Klein, whose name appears on the video artist's underwear or lingerie.[10]

Pre-Text

How are we to play the role of Ganymede to the saintly Jerome in his literary study? And where has he flown to from his perch atop the textual column unfinished by Melencolia? This time, no further than the Media Laboratory at the Massachusetts Institute of Technology.[11] The clock on the wall indicates laboratory time. Our video technology is here carried forward by a mythology that the discipline of theory has yet to identify. Hence Grand Theory in the Human Sciences, (a normally as-sertive and kingly lion in the academic world) is as placid as a lapdog resting on the floor beneath the writing desk of Saint Jerome.

In this high church of technology for today's Saint Jerome, all communications media and technologies are poised for redefinition. Video is a prime component of media merging and converging: televi-sion, telephones, recordings, films, newspapers, magazines, books, and transforming them all, computers. The intellectual kernel of the Media Lab is said by its researchers to be a greater mystery than ever, a grail quest at its highest levels permitting curiosity to prevail over commercial-ity, inasmuch as founding images and their connecting ideas seem to be disappearing over the horizon in every direction. Communication tech-nologies are increasingly interlocked and all-encompassing. When their structure is changing, video is affected. Each time communication means have advanced, the world has experienced metamorphoses. Jerome Weisner, past president at MIT, and his colleagues in the Weisner Building enjoy a reputation of having a clear sense of where their work is going and they commit themselves to it wholeheartedly. If their work has no circumference, it has a center. Hence their writing desks are far more ordered, comfortable, and complete than the Global Village Video Center.

A visit to their laboratory, however, can be a melancholy experience for a video mythographer or critic of video icons. It seems a "video artist" is now looked upon as a "computer peripheral." The reason for this is digitalization, familiar to us all in the forms of the computer disk and the video disk. From graphics to electronics to digitals, computer bits migrate merrily. With digitalization, information in all of the media (radio, television, telephones, printing, recorded music) becomes translatable into each other's codes. Any message, sound, or image may be edited from anything into anything else.

Digitalization presents difficulties, especially for *video vérité* documentaries, in the form of photographic quality. Images on videotape and those synthesized on a computer become identical. What does this mean for electronic news-gathering when the validating function of videotape no longer exists?

Digitalization also presents opportunities. Filmmaking becomes a cottage industry. One craftsman can make a film, instead of significant numbers of technicians. Composite images can save thousands of dollars in location shooting, making the camera into a computer peripheral, not unlike digital sampling in the music business, where you can take any sound and make a virtual instrument out of it, reproducing that sound at any pitch, in any combination, any tempo on a standard electronic keyboard. Suddenly, music history finds itself confronted with the task of redefining all terms of music composition.[12]

Through the current dramatic development of bandwidth compression and somantic data compression techniques at the Media Laboratory, it seems likely the future television set, doubling as a monitor, will not be receiving pictures so much as receiving data and making the pictures. Video theater shows may thus lose their audiences as the camera loses ground to the computer.

On the other hand, what we seem to lose as the eye disappears from behind the camera we may well gain as the eye appears in front of the computerized video screen. Computer technology that makes it conceivable to have eyes as output is called "eye tracking." Developed at the Media Laboratory are "gaze orchestrated dynamic windows," an array of forty simultaneous moving images. Whatever image the viewer looks at steadily, its associated sound track wells up; if interest persists, that image zooms to full size. At the video monitor level, it is exhilarating to think of the possibilities here for Japanese real time and experimental punk video.[13]

There is also a project in spatial imaging that might turn video icons into video truons. It is *medical imaging,* a process in which X-ray-like data from CAP scanners and MRI (magnetic resonance imaging) machines are assembled into three-dimensional images of the body. One peers into a body, peeks around the bone, edits the bone out, and previously obscure structures emerge with remarkable clarity. It's a kind of practice surgery for surgeons and, with different parts of the body, perhaps, a kind of practice poetics for the technology of gender specialists. What is the truon? An imaginary particle vital to interactions involving basic forces of truth; a nice contrast to the computer definition of icons, namely, programs that serve as reminders when you see them and commands when you invoke them.

Digitalization in the video community has not carried the day in all respects. Consider the RCA DVO (digital video interactive), which made a whole hour of full-motion video available on compact disk, thanks to signal compression techniques. The disks did deliver higher quality reproduction and, with a computer attached, any point on the disk can be easily and instantly accessed, a feature impossible with tape. But you could not record as you could with the do-it-yourself magnetic tapes that have captured the home market. Our VCR proletariat, as a courageous underground publisher producing its own videocassettes, matches the verve of the computer subversives of most professions, cheerily leveling institutions of higher learning in particular, promoting students and demoting teachers to appreciated assistants.

If Gutenberg made everyone a reader, Xerox made everyone a publisher, and personal computers made everyone an author, can video production systems make everyone a visionary? Of course, we don't want to be too successful, lest every couch potato in our company turn into a couch fungus. The Media Lab technicians coyly deal with dangers like living with addictive connectivity, total entertainment, out-of-the-body experiences. But in good humor they inflate high-tech only to mock it, seeking to ensure that communications systems are human-based in their very texture.

Science fiction is *the* literature at MIT, thinking what it means to think. I believe the wildly creative side of their incredibly rigorous techniques challenges what video mythographers have been able to learn from literary and art history and criticism. In their humility as scientists, they have been exalted as technologists, inasmuch as computer science compared to physics can be said to be "rotten and ugly." Physics starts with the mathematically beautiful albeit gross trends of systems, and studies them by taking them apart and getting to finer levels of detail. In computer science, quick-and-dirty hackers start with pieces and put them together and look at their implications.[14]

Computers enable programmers to live at the very edge of their intellectual abilities; like the centaurs of myth, they become cyborgs, part human and part machine. In science fiction, if not philosophy of science, they have the salvation of the "alien" going for them.[15] "Demo or die" they say, not publish or perish. Make the case for your idea with an unfaked performance of it working at least once or let somebody else at the equipment. Their focus is invention rather than studies, surveys, critiques. Engineering is a peculiar form of scholarship.

Earlier I mentioned an electronic or poetic gesture or moment or project that commits the whole being of the video artist. I am somewhat chastened by the word "hand-waving" made flesh at the Media Lab. Hand-waving refers to what a speaker does animatedly with his hands as he moves past provable material into speculation, anticipating and overwhelming objection with manual dexterity. Sometimes hand-waving precedes creation, sometimes substitutes for it.

What constitutes healthy communications?[16] Communication ecologists identify equivalents of tides or turbulence or vaporization. We speak today of a cyberspace, where great corporate hotcores burn like neon novas with data so dense that you suffer sensory overload if you try to apprehend the merest outline. Engines without governors rev up and explode. But culturally, I believe we can depend upon mythologies to increase in intensity to maintain humanity's requisite variety. In our wired world, is there not a fable for a teenager with a new car, taking risks, finding new freedoms, whose self-discovery can be a privilege to be around if he's not found on the road some stormy night in an excruciating and tragic traffic accident?

– 8 –

Selling Out "Max Headroom"

Rebecca L. Abbott

Americans came to know a new television personality in 1987 named Max Headroom, although *personality* is perhaps not quite the right word for him. Max first appeared by way of commercials for Coca-Cola as well as in the several books written about and even by him, then on Cinemax, and finally in the short-lived television series produced by ABC in the fall of that year. The TV series represented an unusual climax in the development of this unusual character, a development that brings several issues into focus. For instance, it illustrates how commercial forces can alter and even erase the nuances of the source material they work with; how commercial television can shape and manipulate the values and attitudes of its viewers; and how established cultural forces can absorb and defuse subversive forces in order to make them serve the very power structure these forces are attacking. Because these processes are both subtle and powerful, it is worth taking a closer look at how they work, or worked, in the case of "Max Headroom."

During the spring of 1987, ABC Television developed "Max Headroom" as a four-episode pilot to test the waters for a full-blown series that began, and ended, in the fall of the same year. This rather abrupt ending, however, was the culmination of a complicated evolutionary process that began with an idea of the British television producer, Peter Wagg, to create a computerized character to feature on a music video television series. The creation was meant to be satirical, a parody of talk-show hosts, and Wagg invited Annabel Jankel and Rocky Morton, both noted producers of rock videos, to give the character some life, so to speak. The result was Max Headroom. Morton and Jankel also created a television movie "to explain" his fictional history; Max, like the "replicants" in *Blade Runner*, needed a past in order to have a personality. This movie was entitled *Max Headroom: 20 Minutes into the Future*, and it premiered on British television's Channel 4 in April of 1985. Between the American and British productions, however, a sequence of events transformed the Max phenomenon from his initial role in the 1985 Morton and Jankel "biographical" television movie through the stage of being hot commercial property. This included Coca-Cola's 25 million dollar advertisement campaign ("c-c-c-catch the wave") as well as the combined efforts of Karl Lorimar, Bantam Books, and Vintage Books to ride that wave. This commercial campaign is itself worth examining, for by the time Max was reincarnated for ABC, the transformation of his story was complete.

On the surface, the ABC/Lorimar version of Morton and Jankel's original movie bears a close resemblance to its forbear. In fact, large segments of the original script were retained in the first four episodes of the ABC series, as were many of the special effects images and the two leading actors, Matt Frewer and Amanda Pays. The central plot of both the British film and the American program is set, as its title suggests, in a large urban center "20 minutes into the future" even though, more realistically, its time-frame is several years hence. The city itself is not identified and could be London or New York; the landscape is distinguished only by the advanced degree of urban blight and decay evident everywhere. It is a chilling scenario in which huge, gleaming skyscrapers are intermingled with the gaping ruins and crumbling shells of other buildings. The masses are noisy, violent, boorish, and many are homeless. Perhaps it is a postapocalyptic, post-nuclear vision, but it might simply be a worst-case temporal fulfillment of the kinds of conditions one finds in any modern city today. And while the cause or causes of these conditions is left unspecified, they bear strong resemblance to what we find in recent films such as *Blade Runner*, *The Road Warrior*, and *Brazil*, with the prevalence of surveillance and other control devices strongly reminiscent of Orwell's *1984*. It is a vision of the future world fashioned by a pessimistic projection of the worst trends of contemporary culture.

Both the original film of *Max Headroom* and the American series paint a portrait of an "electro-democracy" completely embedded in technology, totally absorbed in television viewing, and wholly governed by corporate television networks. There are, in fact, 4,000 television channels in this videopolis, with a small number of overarching network/conglomerates fighting to control these viewer-citizens through their television sets.

Central to the story is Network 23, the most successful and popular network with its award-winning news reporter Edison Carter. In both versions of "Max Headroom," Carter discovers during a routine story investigation that Network 23 has been experimenting with a new form of advertisement called a "Blipvert" invented by the corporation's boy genius Bryce Lynch at the bidding of the network's board chairman, which is potentially lethal to certain viewers. The blipvert condenses 30 seconds of advertising to 3 seconds in order to prevent viewers from switching channels during an advertisement. The heightened intensity of brain activity causes the more slothful viewers quite literally to explode.

While ferreting out the truth from Lynch's secret office/workshop, Carter, the reporter, is pursued by thugs whom Lynch has hired. He tries to escape on a motorcycle but he runs into an exit gate marked "MAX HEADROOM 1.3M" and is knocked unconscious. Lynch, the computer whiz, tries to find out if Carter gained access to corporate secrets and, in the tradition of the cinematic Frankenstein, he connects the now comatose Carter's brain to his computer to create a completely computer-generated character based on him. It is this new character who gives the program its name, for in "coming to life" the computer-generated version of Carter can at first only remember what it saw last—the words "max headroom"—which it repeats in a staccato, random fashion, and which Lynch decides to call it.

Taken this far, the story of "Max Headroom" would seem to be a daring and novel subject for a network television series. It suggests that a major network like ABC is responsive to public concern regarding the deteriorating quality of life, urban blight, dehumanization by an allpervasive technology, and fear of totalitarian control of society by corporate interests, especially the fear that corporations will foist anything on the unsuspecting public simply to increase profits.

These, then, are the themes upon which the original film was focused. But in the hands of ABC/Lorimar a strange, but not surprising, series of twists take place. For example, in the original film, once Max has begun to materialize, the chairman of the board of Network 23, Mr.

Grossberg (Mr. "Big City"), makes Lynch dispose of his computer-generated experiment, thinking it is worthless. Max winds up, however, in the hands of an antiestablishment pirate television station called "Big Time TV" (whose slogan is "day after day, making tomorrow seem like yesterday") run by Punks, and he becomes their champion. Not only is Max irreverent and sarcastic, but he knows Network 23's secret about blipverts. He instantly attracts viewers for Big Time TV through his disarming brand of humor, and contributes to the ultimate downfall, by way of a revived Edison Carter, of both Grossberg and Lynch. In short, Max becomes a free agent on the side of the media underground dedicated to combating the stultifying control of Network 23.

In ABC's version, however, Grossberg (now renamed "Grossman") is not put off by Max but takes a liking to him. As Lynch puts it, Max represents the prospect of a "completely programmable news reporter," something for which the network has been longing. But even though Max turns out not to be programmable at all, remaining something of a loose cannon with the ability to roam about at will within the network computer's memory and to unexpectedly appear on screen in order to expose Grossman (as in the original version), he nevertheless remains the puckishly loyal associate of Network 23 devoted to the increase of their ratings. In other words, while Max is certainly a free agent, he is now on the side of the controlling network/corporation. Big Time TV is excised from the script in short order, and with it the singular image of pathos from the original film, which shows forlorn, homeless people sitting huddled amidst the crags of decayed buildings and warmed only by the light of their television sets. Presumably these are the people to whom or for whom Big Time TV tries to speak, but they are excluded in the ABC version. And Lynch, who as he puts it "only invents the bomb but doesn't drop it," becomes friends with Carter and his collaborator Theora Jones (the love interest). These three, then, plus Max, carry out the continuing exploits of Edison Carter's award-winning journalism.

The formula that emerges in the revised ABC version of "Max Headroom" is obviously designed to mold viewer sympathy towards the big network instead of against it as was the case with the original. Moreover, Network 23 is obviously analogous to ABC since it wants to become the biggest network with the highest ratings. Hence the new controlling formula altogether subverts the intent of the original. By preserving the basic setting, characters, and story line of "Max Headroom,"

ABC/Lorimar seduces the viewer into thinking that ABC is truly concerned with the dehumanizing processes that have generated these wretched social circumstances with the implication that ABC somehow stands outside of or is beyond any kind of responsibility for these processes.

The visual style of the American program also conspires to mislead viewers about its thrust. ABC's "Max Headroom" is a faster-paced, slicker version of the British original, but both are highly innovative in style. Wideangle lenses and a very mobile camera are used extensively, again anticipating the visual impact of *Brazil*. "Cinéma vérité" is the hallmark of Network 23, bringing its viewers, and the film's, to news events in progress with the vividness of reality but none of the risk. The editing technique is extremely nimble and rapid fire, creating an almost constant dance between objective and subjective perspectives. Such stylistic videotechnics once again demonstrate, after MTV, "Miami Vice," and numerous TV commercials, the degree to which over 70 years of efforts by experimental filmmakers and more recently video artists have become the conventions of mass cultural fare.

Examined closely, however, one can find several adjustments to eliminate ambiguity and accommodate an ideological transformation. For example, the original film opens with a sequence of ominous shots from surveillance camera perspective, in dull black and white, as Carter's first controller sends him out on assignment. Subsequent shots are from Carter's camera perspective, and it is not until after he has escaped a dangerous situation and come back to confront his cynical colleague that there is a shot in regular, full color from the traditional "objective" perspective, which in itself is a moment of drama. The "moment of drama" is the change from surveillance camera to traditional objective perspective. In the first sequence, the surveillance camera perspectives create a sense of distance for the viewer, the voyeurism that is integral to the motives of the film. Then when Carter gets mugged during the second sequence this intrusive violence is actually heightened since it is seen from Carter's camera perspective, which is taken to be his own—a reporter's experience from inside the action. The violence reaches the viewer very directly.

These subtleties are quite lost in the ABC/Lorimar version, which uses an objective camera perspective indiscriminately throughout the series. When Carter is mugged, the objective camera captures it graphically, and the violent exchange is expanded with extra punches in conventional TV fight-scene style. Later when Carter returns to the network to confront his controller, the drama (controlled in the original) is milked in this version: The single punch he throws is expanded in an exaggerated reverse-angle sequence, and the dramatic moment when he learns that his story was canceled is pumped for all it's worth by way of a long, slow zoom-in to a facial close-up.

Nonetheless, ABC's "Max Headroom" is exciting to watch, and is a real departure from most of network television programming in terms of its visual style. But this is also what makes it so profound a disappointment, and such clear confirmation of the criticism often leveled against commercial television. By making imagery so important, particularly the imagery of "news-making," surveillance cameras, and omnipresent TV screens, ABC seems to be getting ready to tackle some fundamental questions of the effects of mass media on society: the invasion of privacy; mass control through the mass media; the closer and closer bonding between government, business, and media; and even the implications of artificial intelligence, of which Max is an example. But ABC avoids these issues altogether, demonstrating once again how elements of allegedly subversive, probing inquiries directed at the core of the established culture, can be subsumed and contained within a dominant corporate system.

Later episodes of ABC's "Max Headroom" are even more effective at obscuring important but controversial issues. To illustrate, it is again necessary to describe the plot of one of the later programs, which this time has no source in the original British film but is entirely new material.

The fourth episode of ABC's series establishes that one huge central computer controls all the technology of the city in a network that connects electrical, communications, transportation, even plumbing systems: in short, all the functions of the urban environment. Televisions are located everywhere, and it is illegal to turn them off. Voting takes place by computer, instantly, with election outcomes prearranged by the contestants. People who have avoided or refused registration within the central computer are called "blanks" and are considered outlaws. The Orwellian landscape is complete.

The crisis that evolves in this episode has to do with a threat posed by a group of "blanks" who have gained access to the central computer to shut off all of the television sets in the city. The blanks have two demands: they want the release of other blanks who have been imprisoned for evading the system, and they want to stop public manipulation by the "false God" computer/television system.

Edison Carter, Max, and his colleagues, resolve the crisis, naturally, but they arrange a telling compromise. Carter secures the release of the imprisoned blanks by the newly elected government head. But Carter's view is that the masses of people in the city cannot live without TV. "Without their TV's, what is there for them?" he asks, and others agree that "without television this city would be ungovernable." The corrupt, unfeeling, and egomaniacal government head remains in office, Network 23 remains the paternalistic custodian of the "people," controlling them "when it's for the public good." Television remains always on, always present, always shaping and manipulating the public mind.

ABC has certainly played its hand boldly. The cultural values that emerge after watching ABC's "Max Headroom" describe a society split into three classes: government and corporate heads; the poor, boorish, slothful masses; and the intellectual/professional elite of which Edison Carter and Theora Jones are a part. And it falls to the professional class whom Carter, Theora, Lynch and Max represent to defend the interests of the masses, but only insofar as those interests serve the insatiable needs of the corporations. It is a completely hopeless, cynical vision of society that ABC has painted, and its image of the broad masses of the public, which presumably could be equated with the same masses it hoped to court and even serve with "Max Headroom," is devastating.

At this point it is important to address the question of who is responsible for such choices. As Edison Carter himself puts it, "Who is suppressing the story?" This is a key point, and when speaking of ABC as being responsible for the decision to manipulate the plot of "Max Headroom" in order to influence viewers, it is important to note the complex combination of forces at work when a program is planned for network television.

The primary purpose of commercial television, of course, is to sell audiences to advertisers and earn profits for shareholders. Subsumed in that process is the goal of attracting viewers. The networks have always felt the pulse of the public as anxiously as any medical practitioner, although not so much out of concern for the actual health of the patient as from a desire to continue the patient's dependence on their services. Certainly there is much at stake when 30 seconds of prime time sells for anywhere from $80,000 to over $400,000; networks can be expected to do all they can to look out for their interests and those of their sponsors.

The result of their efforts, realized in the programming fare prescribed for their audiences, has been viewer demand of such magnitude that the average American television is on upwards of seven hours per day. This level of saturation has reaped for the caretakers of broadcast television untold rewards in corporate profits. Hence, the medical analogy is not really appropriate, since the treatment is meant to be addictive, not healing.

Within the major networks, the system for determining what programs will be aired is also closely constrained. Hegemonic forces such as the dominant cultural ideology and economic setting, to begin with, establish the particular notions of "common sense" or "normal practice" that underlie the decision-making process.[1] In relation to this, Edward J. Epstein's and Gaye Tuchman's studies of the hierarchies and practices of one aspect of American network production, that of news reporting, are very instructive for demonstrating the degree to which dominant cultural values and assumptions are reinforced in both the process of hiring and promotion of reporters, and in the processes of choosing and investigating actual stories.[2] The pressure to increase ratings and revenues remain major factors.

Beyond that, it is occasionally possible to identify single individuals who are responsible for choices, who make decisions that determine what will appear on air at a scheduled time, and what will not. Av Weston, for example, assumed directorship of ABC News in 1969 (partly in response to Spiro Agnew's attacks on the press), and was given absolute power to oversee, approve, and direct every news story and script before it was aired.[3] He essentially controlled what the audience of the ABC Evening News saw, and described his job this way: "A television news broadcast can be produced in any number of different ways. Every executive producer should have a concept before he begins and it is up to him to translate that concept into the reality of approximately thirty minutes of moving pictures, slides, maps, graphics, anchormen, field correspondents' reports and, hopefully, commercials."[4] So a great deal of responsibility for one network's news can on occasion be located fairly accurately in one individual, if not a group of like-minded ones, and it is reasonable to extrapolate from this that much the same process takes place for purely entertainment programs as well.

In the case of "Max Headroom," one individual who has had great control has been producer Peter Wagg. Certainly his original aims were none other than to create a marketable product. After the tremendous success of *Max Headroom: 20 Minutes into the Future* on Channel 4 in Britain (in the manner of Big Time TV the show doubled their ratings for the time slot), the network went ahead with a weekly talk show and created translated versions for foreign countries.[5] As the character Max grew in popularity (he even had a column in a London entertainment guide) Wagg set his sights on the American market, and it was there where the lucrative Coke contract and other opportunities developed. It was Wagg who persuaded ABC (after both NBC and CBS declined) to agree to an American television series with himself as the executive producer of the program, and Brian Frankish as the producer.

According to Wagg, ABC Entertainment President Brandon Stoddard "told him to make the show his way and that the network would find an audience for it."[6] Nevertheless, changes were made. Wagg felt that "the deliciousness of the show is that a network is allowing us to show how the system works, how ratings are important, why Americans are given the same old material."[7] But what he seems not to have noticed is the degree to which he sold out to that system along the way, extracting the teeth of his watchdog and leaving just its bark. *Newsweek* reported that Wagg was made to cut an entire scene from one episode of the show, apparently because ABC felt it was "too risky" to have a village destroyed by a satellite named Reagan III.[8]

That an established cultural power should harness subversive energies for its own purposes is nothing new, nor is it novel for entrenched forces to paint flaws as strengths. Roland Barthes sees the process of transforming essential weaknesses into positive qualities in this way: "Take the established value which you want to restore or develop, and first lavishly display its pettiness, the injustices which it produces, the vexations to which it gives rise, and plunge it into its natural imperfection; then, at the last moment, save it *in spite of*, or rather by the heavy curse of its blemishes."[9] Stephen Greenblatt has written on the subject of subversive rechanneling in its Renaissance manifestations. In his essay, "Invisible Bullets: Renaissance Authority and its Subversion," Greenblatt demonstrates how a radical interpretation of Moses as a "juggler" or manipulator of Christian faith was actually applied in the service of English colonial interests, in order to manipulate the beliefs of Native Americans so that the Christian God could be wielded over them.[10]

Although it may at first seem far-fetched, the religious analogy is strangely appropriate in the case of Max Headroom. For television in the West has arguably taken the place of religion as the "opiate of the masses." In his multiple incarnations, therefore, Max Headroom might be viewed as some kind of latter-day messiah or a phosphorescent epiphany of warning to the masses. At the very least, it's pretty clear that the star quality of a cult idol is what the makers of the television series were after for their central character, as were those involved with his endorsements. Max Headroom in the British film was the savior of "Big Time TV" and the new and rising champion of the poor and disenfranchised, the blanks who dot the ruins of the countryside sitting in the glow of their TV sets; in ABC's TV series, he was the hero of Network 23 and the masses they claimed to serve. Some might argue that this computer-generated superman could not engender the kind of faith that a true religious leader would, that Max Headroom is no modern Moses, Jesus, or Muhammad. But in an age when charismatic media figures such as Walter Cronkite, Phil Donahue, Johnny Carson and others affect, even shape, the thoughts and lives of millions of followers, Max Headroom can be seen as someone (something?) for whom such status might have been possible. For example, young people quoted in *Business Week* said: "Max is the voice of our generation and someone I trust"; "Max is a cool dude, and people listen to him." And speaking of Coke's mammoth ad campaign, Valeries S. Folkes, professor of marketing at the University of Southern California, said: "With $25,000,000, you can create a whale of a fad."[11]

It was the Coke ads, in which Max was "spokesthing," that did the most to make him a household word in the U.S. Two of these spots were in fact directed by Ridley Scott, director of the recent futuristic films *Alien* and *Blade Runner*. In Scott's creations, vast hoards of young kids chant "Max! Max!" until he appears on screen above them in giant proportions. According to Coca-Cola Senior Vice President John C. Reid, "Max has broken almost every record for awareness of commercials. . . . 76% of all teenagers in this country had heard of Max after our first flight of ads."[12] This approaches the messianic as closely as Madison Avenue usually gets. Beyond this lies the irony of Max Headroom, with his wired, hyper manner of artificial speech, pushing a soft drink containing caffeine and named for the same plant from which cocaine is derived—an allusion probably not lost on many viewers.

Gary Trudeau, creator of the cartoon "Doonesbury," catches the irony in the similarity between Max Headroom and Ronald Reagan. Trudeau invented a character named "Ron Headrest" who bore a striking resemblance to both Reagan and Max Headroom, which reminds us that indeed Reagan is in many ways the Max Headroom of conservative Republicans, and was, at least initially, the messiah of the American middle class. Reagan, the quintessential actor, is a man who was programmed by his political supporters, indeed, given his complete identity, to serve their political agenda. Even his constant glib joking, and slippery "now you see me, now you don't" evasiveness are qualities that bring the ABC/Lorimar Max to mind. The major distinction between the two, of course, is that Reagan has never opposed the dominant cultural ideology in any way whatever; thus it is difficult, if not impossible, to construe him as subversive.

In sum, Max Headroom was converted from an agent of subversion in the Morton/Jankel film to one of controlling ideology in the ABC television series. Since Max was originally designed as a commercial entity, this may most simply explain the agency of transformation. Max was heralded by *Newsweek* as being the first instance of a cult hero who, in the United States, was created "*as a result* of his commercial performances."[13] Certainly his "personality" lent itself to this transformation, for Max was the totally hip, completely outspoken, self-involved and self-adulatory entity entirely geared toward audience response. And while it seems fairly clear that ABC was hoping for real popular success with "Max Headroom," that was not the outcome of their experiment. The meaning of its failure, however, is uncertain. It is not entirely clear that the poor ratings for "Max Headroom" indicate that American television viewers avoided the trap Max Horkheimer and Theodor Adorno predicted for them by not insisting "on the very ideology which enslaves them."[14] And it is puzzling to imagine who ABC was trying to target: the disenfranchised youth subculture that has been loosely associated with the punk movement? The same kids who loved him in the Coke ads? If so, is this an audience that is harder to seduce? Or did the fad simply wear thin? The program had intrinsic flaws, too, aside from its manipulative thrust: it was confusing, and it moved so fast that viewers had trouble following the complexities of the plot. Nevertheless, the fact that ABC made the attempt suggests that they felt there was a chance of success, and in a business where chances are not taken lightly, this signifies something.

It is unfortunate that network television needs to shape its programming so narrowly, because the idea of "Max Headroom" is one that offers wide and fascinating opportunities for exploring a future, highly mediated society. But since the original idea in effect calls for the end of large-scale corporate control of media and culture, it is perhaps too much to ask of a major television network that it dig its own grave. As Blank Reg of Big Time TV announced to the "blank" generation, "You know we said there's no future? Well, this is it!"

– 9 –

What is "Soul"?

Dick Hebdige

What a question!

Many cultural critics today seem fatally fixated on image, on the importance of visual signs, on the ascendancy and dominance of visual media. Various effects are imputed to TV, and such effects tend to be assumed rather than proven.

TV is pictured as a ruinous intrusion: a monster in the home. The influence of the TV cyclops is seen to be massive and invidious. In those streams of cultural commentary that present themselves as "serious" and "responsible," both inside and outside the academy, TV is more often than not accused of supplanting the family as primary socializing agent, of indoctrinating the viewer—the unprotected viewer—with false goals and values proffered by dubious role models, and by surreptitiously promoting compliance with the dominant ideology. TV is thus routinely invested by concerned intellectuals everywhere with fabulous powers. The viewer is depicted as silently absorbed, and this viewer is always *other* to the critic, who has access to superior knowledge and an exalted vantage point, the point from which the critic's demystifying critique itself is undertaken.

This silently absorbed, ideal-average viewer tends to be presented as floating outside any specific historical or social context, as a pair of disembodied eyes, as a spectator. This tends to be the case whether the viewer in question is the passive dope or dupe of mass culture theory, a cipher for the culture industry "slumped" (the serious critic's favorite verb) in front of "the box". Or, to switch to that amalgam of semiotics and psychoanalytic theory now institutionalized in communications courses, at least in Britain, as the radical alternative, the spectator is presented as "a function of the text," as the unwitting "subject" of ideology "positioned" by the unmarked, hence insidious, operations of the text. Military metaphors abound in serious TV criticism: TV is said to "invade" and "bombard" us with imagery. The viewer is, or so the argument goes, "overwhelmed," "swamped," and "saturated." The implication is that the image-consumer is mesmerized and then seduced, laid out and then laid low. Such descriptions and analyses of inferred audience response and reader-text relations are bound together by the critics' resolve to substitute vigilance for pleasure, to exchange consciousness and cognition for unconsciousness and recognition/identification. They are bound together by the critic's determination to keep the critical response separate from, and radically opposed to, the vulgar responses of the untutored audience (vulgar from *vulgus*, "the people").

And running underneath that as a kind of unifying thread, a thread that ties the professional (by that I mean the paid intellectual) back to his or her antique origins in the priesthood: a profound antipathy to visual representations with identifiable referents, specifically a fear of figuration and of mirrors, an antipathy seeded at the very root of the dominant traditions within western thought. This antipathy is linked to the Platonic downgrading of sensory experience, to the Platonic distinction between the palpable/imperfect and impalpable/eternal, between real and ideal forms, the visible world and the invisible beyond. It is linked as well perhaps to the ancient Hebrew prohibition on graven imagery, where man, created in the *selem* or the image of God as caretaker and lord of the rest of creation, is forbidden from producing the *icon*, the form or statue, or the *demut*, the likeness, the replica. Iconography here appears intrinsically, implacably at war with the True and the Good. Video icons *versus* values, in some accounts of what has come to be called the post-modern condition, video icons versus the very notion of value itself.

Post-modernity and post-modernism are the late twentieth century buzzwords for contemporary crisis or emergency: crisis surrounding the old institutionalized hierarchies of value. Crisis in the old strong model of critique, where the image of the artistic avant-garde, as an army of soldiers battling away at the borders of the visible, is no longer regarded as viable; the radical intellectual vanguard no longer presumes to divine and engineer the collective future. Crisis, in other words, of authority and political direction: a sense of exhaustion in the old artistic and critical languages, a sense of the difficulty of imagining a future when history itself sometimes appears to have vanished, flattened out behind us by the power of corporate capital, by the machinations of the big multinationals, by computational simulation and mass media. Flattened out, too, by the implosion of meaning and any sense of the real as given and bounded, the real as set apart from and prior to representation. It's often said we live in deadly times—the death of art, death of values, death of the Enlightenment faith in reason and representation, in the sense both of political representation (for instance, when someone stands up and says I speak for these others, represent their interests) and representation in the more general sense of signs having stable, identifiable referents out there. It amounts to the death of the Great Metanarratives, the end of narrative closures, the end of story. Get the picture? Apocalypse Now.

And talking of pictures, take pop art as a post-modernist project. The long line of modernist avant-gardes within the arts beginning in the late nineteenth century sought in one way or another to get underneath the surface of things through abstraction, through the exploration of two-dimensionality on canvas, the abandonment of Renaissance perspective and the illusionism of the frame as window; to get beneath the surface through defamiliarization, through the provocative gestures of the dadaists and situationists or by deploying the "overviews" and "insights," the corrosive apparatus of Marxian critique (exposing, say, through photomontage, the underlying generative structures, the real relations concealed beneath the mystifying layer of appearance); to get beneath appearance by unleashing in surrealist art and Dada the subversive troubling power of the unconscious. Pop art by contrast jettisons all of that serious, anxious straining beyond the given and the immediate, that searches for personal authenticity and original insight. Instead what we get in pop is the fascination of commodities, of surfaces and mirrors. Seen from this perspective, pop becomes the only properly post-modernist gesture, for in pop we see the capitulation of painting to television and advertising, the end of the brush-as-weapon-and-scalpel, the end of the artist as engineer of the future, as soldier and as surgeon, cutting out the problems of the masses—whether the problem be defined as false consciousness proper (mystification of the power/wealth axis) or the dogged persistence with which real people go on preferring Michael Jackson to Jackson Pollock—end of the singular painterly mark. In its place we get the smooth surface of the photographed or silk-screened reproduction, the end of the artist as-critic-of-the-seen: S-E-E-N. Instead, what we get is the fascinated complicit gaze of the artist-as-consumer, the artist as tape-recorder, as celebrity and star. In Warhol's words: "If you want to know about Andy Warhol, just look at the surface of my paintings and films and me and there I am. There's nothing behind it." Pure exclusive surface—end of what Fredric Jameson calls "the depth model."

Even where the I/eye, where centered subjectivity is itself questioned, decentered or historicized, the old economy of the sense prevails. Jean Baudrillard suggests we are living in the age of the simulacrum—but even there, in this kind of critique, the focus is predominately visual; there is a preference for examples and figures drawn from the field of visual perception. Even in Foucault, even in Derrida, the tendency is to privilege sight over the other senses, to privilege the visual apprehension of spatial relationships. Think of Foucault's preoccupation with the "voir" in *savoir/pouvoir*; with technologies of surveillance, the omnipresent eye of power. Think of Derrida's emphasis on the *trace*, the written sign over speaking and the metaphysics of presence, the emphasis on *différance*—the double process of differing and deferring inscribed within all utterance.

In the post-modern apocalypse, where everything dies (from meaning, art and authorship, to God, the Subject and the *grands récits*), the ear remains a relatively neglected organ. Yet to listen to the world instead of setting out heroically to read it, to acknowledge that it may be more appropriate, more honest and in the long run more fruitful to remain confused,

>   —confused in *the shadow of the object*

>   rather than trying

>   to aggressively master it,

>   to decipher its significance, to interpret it,

>   to break it down, refer it up to

>   preexistent general frameworks of significance—this listening in the shadow of the object might offer something new. New kinds of knowledge might become available to us, more suggestive tentative and open-ended forms of critique might grow out of such an encounter. To linger, listening in the shadow of the object, involved in its complex-

ities and confused by them, by the densely layered nature of our responses, our relations to the object.

In the words of Jacques Attali we are today everywhere confronted by the "bankruptcy of the gaze." He writes: "For twenty-five centuries, Western knowledge has tried to look upon the world. It has failed to understand that the world is not for the beholding, it is for hearing, it is not legible, but audible."[1]

Such a shift in the "ratio of the senses" might also entail a shift within the episteme, it might (who knows?) inaugurate a less paranoid, less power-driven, more equitable and horizontally organized economy of sense. New principles of hope might be resurrected within such a transformed economy.

For Walter Ong, sound is distinguished by its evanescence. "It is not simply perishable but essentially evanescent, and is sensed as evanescent. When I pronounce the word 'permanence,' by the time I get to the '-nence,' the '*perma-*' is gone, and has to be gone."[2] Evanescent, bound into time, sound also has a unique relationship to interiority—unique when compared with that of the other four senses—because we can register interiority through hearing without violating the integrity of the form under focus, without murdering to dissect. You can ring a coin to establish what metal it's made of, you don't have to melt it down. Sound implies a center and a depth and Ong takes the comparison with sight further:

> Sight isolates, sound incorporates. Whereas sight situates the observer outside what he views, at a distance, sound pours into the hearer. Vision dissects. . . When I hear, however, I gather sound simultaneously from every direction at once: I am at the centre of my auditory world, which envelopes me, establishing me at a kind of core of sensation and existence. . . . By contrast with vision, the dissecting sense, sound is thus a unifying sense. A typical visual ideal is clarity and distinctness, a taking apart. . . . The auditory ideal, by contrast, is harmony, a putting together.[3]

We fail to listen at our own peril. We should not lose sight of the auditory ideal, the binding power of sound, the binding power of the living speaking voice. TV and video after all, operate in two dimensions, in sound as well as image. What I am emphasizing here is the need to *attend* to music video, to listen and to look, to concentrate as much on the aural-oral plane as on the reader-text relation, on listening and looking.

In *Noise: The Political Economy of Music*, Jacques Attali offers a model and a method to develop this attention. His model presents music as organized noise and prophetic noise. Music is prophetic noise "because it explores much faster than material reality can, the entire range of possibilities in a given code. It makes audible the new world that will gradually become visible, that will impose itself and regulate the order of things; it is not only the image of things but the transcending of the everyday, the herald of the future."[4]

Attali's method is to regard his book as a "call to theoretical indiscipline," and he stresses at the outset his intention not only to theorize about music but to theorize *through* music. What I am aiming at, then, is a kind of rhapsody, a weaving or stitching together of images and sounds (from the Greek *rhapsoidein*, meaning to "rhapsodize," literally to "stitch songs together").

Whether soul is conceived as source of vital energy, as the capacity for self-volition; as that which sinks or falls into the flesh; as the occupying force or spirit which penetrates, inspires, occupies, and animates the body; whether opposed to the flesh or distinguished from but not opposed to it, whatever else it is or isn't, its one defining characteristic is that it cannot be seen. "Soul" from the Old English *sawol* means "life," the spiritual or emotional part of man linked to the Greek *aiolos* meaning "quick-moving" or "easily moved." In the Hebrew Bible where the human being is conceived as a single psychosomatic entity, an intimate and indivisible mingling of *nephesh* ("soul"), *ruah* ("spirit") and *basar* ("flesh"), the word *nephesh* has an unusually rich and complex connotative range, embracing at different points the meanings "desire," "appetite," the "center of any living organism," and hence the "person." The literal meaning is apparently "gate of breath," by metonymy, breath itself, the act of breathing. As Gaston Bachelard, philosopher of science and phenomenologist of space, of reverie and fire, wrote in *The Poetics of Space*: "The word Soul is an immortal word. In certain poems it cannot be effaced for it is a word born of our breath." He cites Charles Nodier, who wrote in 1828 that "The different names for the soul among nearly all peoples are just so many breath variations and onomatopoeic expressions of breathing."[5]

"The breath is the *pneuma*," writes Roland Barthes. "The soul swelling or breaking" as he seeks to distinguish it from what he calls the "grain" of the voice, the body in the voice, the irreducibly particular, material trace, to distinguish *phenotype* from *genotype*. Breath, the mythology of presence, the bearer of the Word, holy stuff and medium of life, ethereal because invisible, intangible, impalpable, *breath* sweet or odorless (ideally at least) and contrasted thus with all the other bodily emissions.

Soul in, not of, the body carried on the breath. Unrepresentable, beyond figuration, always moving out of sync. It cannot be mimed or held or reproduced. It flies out of frame. Watch Mahalia Jackson's mouth as she sings another person's soul out of this world in the closing minutes of Douglas Sirk's "Imitation of Life." The lips slip out of sync. The soul flies out of focus. Soul equals soul music: a fusion of African-American R&B and African-American gospel, the vocal testifying styles, the close harmonies, the melisma, the call and response structure of gospel transposed to the field of popular music. Soul in sound and music is the investment of popular song with the excess of feeling and the degrees of intensity associated with acts of devotion and prayer. Soul music is defined by the songwriter Don Covay as "total vocal freedom": total vocal freedom to cross and blur and stretch the lines between the sacred and the secular, church and stage, the pillow and the pulpit, the death bed and the love bed.

The problem is with performance—with enactment, reenactment, the repetition and replication of a performance. How does one distinguish the authentic, the genuine from its treacherous shadow? Performance: the manufacturing of effects, the manipulation of affect, scripted, scored in advance. For the ancient Greeks music possessed divine, daemonic powers, stirring and moving the listener against the listener's will (myth of Orpheus), weaving the power of enchantment (the Sirens' threat was immaculate seduction of seamen through the ear). Singing—deceptively sincere—as a casting of spells—S.I.N.C.E.R.E.

Soul music: essence of the "live," the singer's voice trapped within the 12-bar structure, beating up against the bars. The dissolve into pure utterance.

Repetition. Pure aspiration: the going beyond language, the breathing out of sound beyond words: the spectacle of language collapsing underneath the weight of what is there to be expressed.

The voice drowned in tears.

Nowadays soul music is returned, rerun on TV in advertising as sign of the finest purest hour of Teen. Reimaged, repackaged and recut. Soul to sell us Levi Jeans.

Recut on classic lines: a police siren laid out on the falling curve of a line from an old Ben E. King song. The pleasure of remembering and imagining is stitched into the denim. Soul has congealed into a secondary commodity: something to sell something else with.

The contest between sound and image, listening and reading can be staged in a playful way by looking at, listening to, and loosening up some of the questions posed by pop promo video clips. That contest is already staged at an intrinsic level in the form of pop video. It is hardly surprising that pop video has already received a great deal of attention in post-modern critique and in definitions of post-modernism, where it functions as symptom or exemplar of various shifts in the political economy of signs and sounds.

The impact of video on popular music has tended to be viewed negatively by professional rock critics. The image is said to contaminate the sound, to preempt and channel the potential imaginative investments made on the part of the audience, to limit the capacity of individual listeners to integrate popular music into their personal biographies, to supply their own imaginaries, to make sense of the music for themselves. They are said to consolidate the power of both the big name artists at the expense of minority musics and of the big multinational record companies at the expense of the independents, because of the prohibitive production costs and the sometimes explicitly racist programming policies of the (cable) music companies.

The rise of video promos has been seen as part of a long-term decline in the live context, which is considered to provide a minimum guarantee for the preservation of popular music's vitality, authenticity, rough edges, and capacity to attract raw talent against the standardization of product. From this perspective, rock videos concentrate yet more attention on the visual dimension and distract attention away from the authentic flow of utterance in the singer's voice and in the unpredictable, unstable contexts of live musicianship. Promo videos are thus seen as a further commodification of music into packaged product in a process that leads to the primacy of the televisual: the simulacrum. This tendency and its obverse (the nostalgia for the real, the live, the direct unmediated access to the presence of the performer which rock, jazz, blues and soul have always promised) is clearly visible in the persona of a star like Bruce Springsteen whose live performances in gigantic auditoriums are only made possible thanks to the most elaborate lighting, mixing, and amplification technologies. Springsteen's performances are hyper-live. He performs accompanied by his own image projected onto a huge screen behind him. His image, his presence, and his power—power to represent the real America—are thus amplified along with the music. Pop promos are seen actively to assist in this process whereby the line between originality and simulation dramatically disintegrates. They are sometimes seen as monstrous hybrids—neither "pure entertainment" nor "pure promotion"—where the image and the sound, the video and the record chase after each other (i.e., sell each other) in a double helix that short-circuits other possibilities (e.g., contact with the real, the audience, the street). Active fandom, public audience participation and dialogue between performers and record buyers are replaced by passive consumption of industrial product in the private context of the home.

MTV, set up in August 1981 by Warner Inc. together with its corporate partner American Express, delivers people in their early teens to early twenties, the young and young at heart—that is, those who have yet to develop fixed consumption patterns—to the advertisers. MTV is thus an attractive proposition for advertisers of products like Coca-Cola, jeans, candy, shampoo, etc., because it breaks with the wide net broadcasting strategies that still dominate national network TV in the United States. MTV is about narrow-casting and niche-marketing, not broadcasting. It targets a particular segment of the audience, defining that segment and beaming in exclusively on it so that Coca-Cola can get direct access to their market: the Pepsi Generation, as their rivals call it, young people of all ages everywhere. MTV executives are apparently fired with a mission: to transform viewing habits, to produce new rituals and forms of consumption, to cultivate a new relation between the viewer and TV, a new attitude less consciously wired for meaning and message, more distracted, yet receptive. In the words of John Marks, a Canadian music video executive, "We want people to use the TV as an electronic fireplace. With MTV they leave the set on when people are around where they wouldn't normally leave a TV set on."

The music promo converges with the TV commercial in terms of cost, of primary function and of form (rapid jump-cuts, cannibalization of existing formats, rapid edits aimed at holding the 3 1/2-minute attention span). Formally the pop promo videos rely less and less heavily on the televisual codes evolved in broadcast TV in the sixties and seventies, codes designed to maximize the sense of excitement and the impression of immediacy associated in the representation of pop and rock music with live performance. There is a genre of pop video, the performance video, which remains more or less tied to those codes, but there is also at the same time a pulling-away from the straightforward recording and relay of a one-off event: the concert.

In a recent Run DMC and Aerosmith video, for example, a mock battle is staged between what appear to be radically opposed musical forms, performance, and consumption styles: the "live" codes of white rock, the second-order rap and scratch of black hip-hop, baroque white boys versus cool black boys, Mick Jagger simulacrum versus Malcolm X squared. The contest is playfully resolved as *everybody* learns to walk and talk this way. The violence is directed solely at the walls separating genres, audiences, and markets, at the wall that kept black rap off MTV throughout the early 1980s.

As pastiche and the deliberate orchestration of intertextual codes take over in video promos, they contribute to that process whereby TV is said to cannibalize and turn in upon itself against the old televisual aspiration to present a window on the world. The defining characteristic of pop promos might be summed up as the substitution of referential density for narrative coherence.

In this kind of pop promo, indexical signs—those motivated signs which move the narrative along—succumb to referential signs (those signs which evoke atmosphere, establish mood, give clues to "character"— clothing, postures, lighting, special effects, etc.). In this way, the pop promo video becomes a form *designed to tell an image* (the image of the band) rather than to tell a story (the story of a particular event, a particular performance). The overall implication seems to be that flatness rules, and that flatness rules *forever* in the monumental indifference of TV as it absorbs and thereby negates all of history, meaning, value. But that, perhaps, is to look and not to listen. We may find evidence of a contrary flow when we seriously endeavor to unglue the soundtrack and the imagetrack.

And then . . . the return of soul: soul music. Since the mid-eighties, Britain has been enjoying a soul revival: sixties' Atlantic soul, early seventies' funk, forties' and fifties' bebop, cool- and hard-bop jazz and gospel music have become the lingua franca of the street, at least in the inner city. I do not mean just a physical or cultural location so much as that part of the city inhabited as dreamscape and as myth-site by people who might live outside actual cities in small towns, say, or in suburbs. Not Muzak, not rock, not even the rocky hard-edged avalanche of rap, but rather the rhapsody of soul. In the sometimes obsessive and increasingly costly search for "rare grooves," the soul fans comb the racks of the secondhand record shops tracking down rare old funk and soul discs. We could speculate on the reasons for this craze: the general preoccupation with nostalgia and recycling, the impact of those Levi's ads. Or alternatively, impatience with pop, with video, with surface, and with the packaging of style. Soul is a means of articulating a new community of affect—*articulating* in the double sense of linking with and expressing, positioning and bringing forward into being. Soul and the nostalgia for the real. Soul as a way of making sense—personal and collective sense—in a way that is active, and actively opposed to the kinds of sense that are dominant and given. Soul as a way of building back a sense of ground and holding that ground against a sense of weightlessness and vertigo, against the dizzy centripetal pull of what Baudrillard calls the "ecstasy of communication." The industry is now beginning to rerelease rare grooves to catch the new soul buffs, and of course it is only a matter of time before the momentum is halted and brought within the steadier more controlled rhythms of exchange and distribution favored by the big record companies. But then there will be the turning away to somewhere else. Soul music: revenge of the depth model.

That is an alternative reading from the readings cited earlier, anyway. Perhaps it might be better described as a different kind of listening—a listening rather than a watching, an attending to textures, not a reading of texts. The beating of time, the beating-back in time on history: Music has always served this function of storing up and passing on shared histories, of binding together communities. Such functions are especially developed within the African, the African-American, and African-Caribbean traditions where music welds together what Paul Gilroy calls an "interpretive community" dispersed in the diaspora.[6] Here rhythm and recording technologies are used to conserve a sense of history: In rap, jazz and dub reggae, quotation is used to make the past *audible in the present*, so that history is recovered, and reworked in a dialogic process which asserts a sense of collective destiny, shared roots, and common interests for people whose historical being has been consistently and systematically denied. In scratching, the record becomes a percussive instrument in its own right. The technology of sound is seized in time and used as an instrument of empowerment. The voices of the past, recorded speeches of the black leaders—Martin Luther King, Malcolm X—have been brought back from the grave, retrieved from the sound archives by artists like Bobby Womack and Keith Leblanc and resurrected, put into the mix on recent dance records.

There is value in repetition. In returning a voice, in mobilizing the power of the already said against the inertia of the past. We are still talking here about the articulation of identity and desire; about identities formed across assemblages comprised of commodities; identities formed, if you like, *through consumption*. *Consumption*, though, with its connotations of waste, of using up, and devastation, seems inappropriate and inadequate given that this taking up of commodities, this relishing of the sumptuary act also invokes a kind of devotional element, a polishing-up of the object (buffing), a libidinal investment on the part of the consumer. We are talking here about forms of persistence (these are second-hand records) and of effects that linger (we might say we find such records haunting). Time is inscribed on the very surface of the object as a material presence in the form of scratches. Some old records sound as though someone were tap-dancing all over them, the patina of time laid across their very surface: the history of their uses and abuses.

The word "subculture" does not adequately designate the forms of affiliation I'm trying to sketch out here. Larry Grossberg's term "affective alliances" comes much closer:[7] alliances of affect binding together groups and individuals who may be segregated temporally or spatially, affective alliances that can no longer be returned to preestablished communities as they tend to be traditionally conceived, i.e., as static, god-given, arboreal; rooted, say, in sexual preference, ethnic origin, occupation, social class, or territory.

The ground I'm talking about can't be seen or shown like that. It has to be listened for. It's plastic, synthetic. It's in the air, in the airwaves. It is more of an inclination, a tilting that directs flows of yearning, that can at times achieve a pitch and an intensity that becomes almost palpable. Soul.

There comes a point in certain kinds of music, in certain types of singing and in our encounter with that music and that singing, where the desire for deliverance and completion, the desire to step across the border, to get across to the other side, becomes so intense, when the loss and the longing get so mixed-up, that it's impossible to decide as you listen to the song or the snatch of music whether the yearning is for Zion or for a lover, for oceanic self-annihilation or absorption in the other. At such times these different kinds of qualities of yearning—the yearning for a lover, for deliverance from pressure—become fused, cojoined. As the listening body and the listener's breath are drawn into the grain of the sound at the center of the song or snatch of music, as these two lines of intensity converge inside the listening, breathing body, they find a focus, an opening there, an indication that points . . . nowhere . . . and that pulls us in that direction (we might say that the record turns us inside out).

"Nowhere" is another name for utopia (etymologically, the word *utopia is* derived from the Greek *ou* meaning "no," and *topos* meaning "place"). We shall have to listen *out* for utopia, to move forwards into nowhere, remembering the route we've travelled, and where we've come from, beating back in time, beating back on history . . . back, I suppose, to the irreducibility of lived experience, to the power of testimony and witness, to the seizing of the time, to the snatching of the means to give voice—to speak out in time, the bitter-sweet process of re-membering.

– 10 –

An Afterword: Beyond Lamentation

Christopher Parr and Debra Parr

Video as Listening Post

The appealing sense of "nowhere" which Dick Hebdige's account of "Soul" (Chapter 9) works towards—the "nowhere" *(outopos)* he urges us to listen out for, to listen back to—receives more elaborate articulation in his discussion of a rock music video by the eccentric but popular American band, Talking Heads. Their song, and the video created for it by the band's lead singer and conceptualist, David Byrne, is felicitously titled "Road to Nowhere." The written text of Hebdige's discourse, framed by a series of stills from the video, can be found in his book *Hiding in the Light: On Images and Things*, as the last of four "postscripts," four characterizations of what he calls "the Post."[1]

Two of this video's qualities in particular affirm for Hebdige ways in which "nowhere" may be the most soulful and significant place for us to live in a world dominated by the post-modern sublime and its attendant alienations. The first is the video's confident ease with fragmentation, its enactment of the viability of vitality in the face of our television-image culture's appetite for slicing, dicing, disintegration, and cannibalism. There's a buoyancy to its plethora of rapid cuts, image repetition, and quick witted quotation of iconography, high and pop, symbolic and inane. This buoyancy treats the "road to nowhere" not as austere retreat nor dessicated wasteland, but as a place divertingly, if not comfortably, habitable. Describing the effect of the frenetically crazy animated passage towards the end of the video, Hebdige writes:

> We get stuck for the time being on the crazy ride, the fairground ride, the signifying whiplash where we slide along the signifiers from one circle to the next as we recapitulate our passage through the life-cycle from a birthday cake with candles on it and a smiling Mr. Friendly face at one end, to a bleeding world and water going down the plug hole at the other end.
>
> But it's alright, the Talking Head tells us. It's all right.[2]

The second quality Hebdige admires, the one that helps make it "all right," is laughter:

> For what marks the Talking Heads' tape off from modernism—what puts it firmly in the Post—is that it has a light and laughing touch. . . . What makes it Post is that you can have fun with it: it is, as Byrne himself says, "multileveled": you can dance to it, enjoy the undemanding rhythm, think about its "message(s)," read it allegorically, use it as you like. You can watch it and forget it or steal it off the airwaves via video and play it back as often as you like."[3]

But for all its insight and willingness to reevaluate video and popular culture, *Hiding in the Light*, being a text in a book illustrated with black-and-white photos, remains a "reading." As such, it is bound (as all the chapters in this book similarily are) to the visual, verbal, and conceptual habits of reading texts. Hebdige's lecture-presentations are something else. And it is in them that we may begin to see how his sense of 'listening' can shape an alternative to "readings" and to their pedagogic equivalent, the "lecture"—with all the senses of authority, authorship and mastery that term entails. His performance-presentations offer a method and a model for the engagement of complex cultural artifacts so as to learn from them, to include them in the mix, in the shifting groundswell of our human being.

Using a double slide-show, video, film, and tapedeck, Hebdige invites a kind of listening that might produce several effects if practiced in the university, even on a very small scale. He stands on the stage in relative darkness, calling on the eye, but also on the ear for information. In a move reminiscent of Walter Benjamin's separating the aural from the visual in film, Hebdige unglues the soundtrack from the image, never evoking the "profound antipathy to visual representation" that he locates at the root of western forms of thought and discourse, yet determined to work around and through "the bankruptcy of the gaze." These multimedia performances clearly disclose the method of their construction: a kind of wild-style pastiche of image and sound and written text that are evocative of historical specificities defining the present moment. Music, industrial noise, breath, sighing, laughter, patois, clatter, and other instances of the aural debris and undertones of this technological civilization and its many forebears are ingeniously summoned forth. Hebdige finds in them wellsprings for deepening our understanding of the historical lived experiences that our image-culture now appears only to plunder for its own gain, and from them he suggests certain possibilities for Soul we might draw out of the groundswell. The audience's attention is drawn to music or sounds, and they are encouraged to make of it what they will ("He who has ears to hear, let him hear"), to incorporate or harmonize themselves with the melody, threnody, or cacophony of recorded moments.

Thus, in performance, what Hebdige means by 'listening' amplifies what he makes of the Talking Heads' video. He actively demonstrates his desire for "trying to move away from what I feel increasingly to be an inappropriate analogy between dealing intelligently with popular culture, and 'reading' it, since I find this reduction of our relation to the world to a reading of texts increasingly constraining and unsatisfactory."[4] Instead, he jogs "alongside Mr. Byrne," as he puts it, "down the road to nowhere for awhile," using the video clip as a pretext "to climb inside it, to return a voice." The voice he calls back to is Byrne's as it "suddenly flies up into a higher, more desperate/ecstatic register," at the point alluded to earlier, of "impossible animation . . . the stream of swirling circle images." Hebdige's response itself achieves, even in written form, "a pitch and intensity that becomes almost palpable" (Chapter 9, this book, p. 132), not masterfully analyzing, but sounding out in poetic terms the *textures* of Talking Heads' image swirled music.

Even while he describes visual imagery, Hebdige is antiphonally answering the upbeat tone and rhythms of the sound track. Still more noteworthy is how performance allows him to convey dramatically his point about laughter. Using precisely the technology that allows teachers as much as dub/reggae producers to slice into music, to "plunder" a predecessor's work, he intersperses his commentary with the laughter of exemplary voices, activating the text in a way barely glimpsed in *Hiding in the Light*. Although we can only name names here, not splice in the laugh tracks, the draft or score of his performance of this piece will convey something of how he works. Speaking of how the Road to Nowhere is where we are and all there is for us to get on with, he continues:

> The realisation can produce laughter—not the artful snigger of the enfant terrible, John Lydon also known as Johnny Rotten . . . [He *plays Lydon's laugh*] . . . not the hollow savage laughter, the derisive laugh of the avant garde, the machiavellis, the Malcom McLarens of this world . . . [He *plays McLaren's laugh from "Boys' Chorus" on the Fans LP*] . . . but something closer to a belly laugh, a pregnant laugh. . . . When we set up home on the road to nowhere we may have to learn to laugh our way around whatever sense of dread and crisis may afflict us, to laugh through the grave times we are living through.
>
> That would mean learning to laugh not carelessly but CARE-FULLY, because *everything* is still at stake, everything is still to be made over . . . [He *plays Patsy Cline's laugh from "Loving You"*][5]

The gist of Hebdige's take on (music) video as resource and metonym for contemporary culture, evident in his discussion's opening paragraphs as much as in the laughter just quoted, is that the outlook is not all bad if we have the resilience to adapt, to question our expectations and our favored methodologies. His is a questioning of how we arrive at our values. It amounts to a call to come to all our senses, especially to listen rather than just to look (or gaze, or read, or stare, or simply go blind).

He thus strikes a chord with our own sense of what it means to be part of a culture already transformed by video: the necessity that educators and intellectuals alike get beyond lamentation, beyond the sense of violation, of being forced into an unwelcome and unwelcoming arena, beyond the sickening sense of vertigo that the ground has gone from under us, that we have lost any grip on our children, that we will not recognize where we are already. In particular, it may be very valuable to get beyond nostalgia for some time when the literary, philosophical, and religious canons were (supposedly) in their place and all was right with the world. If death, that buzzword Dick Hebdige has already mockingly challenged, is an appropriate metaphor for the loss or passing away of that world, it may not be a death worth lamenting.

Video Culture, Video Germs

A recent television commercial for an airline begins with high-speed, rapid-cut footage of a fellow jerking his way through a typically hectic American airport to the accompaniment of some electronic rock music beating out, New Order, Depeche Mode or the like. A voice-over intones on the unpleasantness of most air travel, which the viewers are meant to take as being portrayed aurally and visually before them. But, the voiceover tells us, air travel doesn't have to be like that.

Abruptly a distinct change occurs in how the same imagery is filmed and edited: the music becomes easy listening, and the cuts, angles, and pace of the clips becomes "smooth," that is, they conform to the familiar transitions and predictable conventions of standard American television. The voice-over tells us that this particular airline ensures that your trip is reassuringly smooth, comfortable, relaxing.

The striking thing about this ad for us is that it is the earlier sequence that appeals, catches our attention, comes across as exciting and desirable, in contrast with the banal and predictable moves of the second half. In this we are responding as anyone who enjoys innovative rock videos might. We do like airline travel to be reassuring and relaxing—but we're watching a video, not an airport. It is clever appropriations from rock videos that make television ads like this stimulating, worthwhile, rather than merely an interruption or opportunity to switch channels.

To be living on the text/video cusp is to find oneself, ready or not, in a complex and disorienting arena, where the iconography of a Marilyn Monroe movie made before most rock video viewers were born can be employed by a young woman named for the Mother of Jesus to depict her ostensible status and desirability as a "Material Girl"—or a young viewer's familiarity with jump cuts, synthesized drumming and distorted imagery can subvert an airline's appeal to satisfaction based on "followability" (in Ricoeur's sense of that term), a principle deemed essential in 5000 years of traditional narrative. A friend of ours, high school age, tells of going into a record store with a school friend. A display over the door featured two album covers, The Clash's *London Calling,* and Elvis Presley's 1956 album *Elvis Presley.* "Oh look," says the friend, bristling with contempt, "Elvis copied The Clash." Such temporal and symbolic disorientations, along with the confused expectations that accompany them, are pervasive. Numerous youth movies depend on and use versions of TV rock music and their composition techniques. So do ads, and several popular television shows. If one looks for where to find models of youth self-identity, music videos and their spinoff movies and ads are clearly one of the first places to go.

To teach by texts alone therefore doesn't appear an option for many of us entering the teaching profession in the 1990s, who have ourselves lived entirely in the "age" of television and rock 'n' roll. To cultivate "Culture" in those already acculturated in the video culture, calls us into the role of being a medium among media. We need to devise ways of so being, to discern values among the icons, rather than opt out through a sense of cultural superiority. The fairly simple example above of the airline ad is only a minor instance of how 'listening' to video, to its sounds, its images and its rhythms, may be a start: a means of responding to—and resisting— what television culture wants of us. It also hints at a consequent revaluation of values: the 'listening' urged by Dick Hebdige will likely lead us to incorporate what our traditional cultural values experience as NOISE—disruptive, disjunctive, disturbing, dysfunctional.

Listening in this way can lead to learning, especially when artistic creativity appears, deliberately or unexpectedly, on the small screen. The American artist Robert Longo, friend and associate of other media-image-influenced artists such as Cindy Sherman, David Salle, and Nancy Dwyer (all of them progeny of pop in the lineage of art's -isms) has made a video for the British post-punk band New Order. The song is called "Temptation," the video "Bizarre Love Triangle." It is a sophisticated piece of videomaking, with a lot of very rapid-cut footage, computer-generated abstract and geometric imagery, altered speeds, split-screen images and complex post-production effects. Watching it, one is aware of a great amount of creativity contained within a 4.10 minute fragment. First there is New Order's music, a combination of multiple synthesizer technology and coordination, more conventional rock music composition, and evocative lyrics. Then there are Longo's visuals, working very provocatively between the common stock of the rock video genre(s), and his own art. He draws on both his fascinating series of portraits *(Men In Cities)* of bodies dressed in suits, their seemingly contorted postures suspended against blank backgrounds, and on his large constructions where an image, often flattened or horizontally elongated, is overshadowed by a quite dissociated image or shape two or three times its size looming above it. At their best these constructions are geometrically quite disorientating, unsettling. On a small screen the physical disturbance is less strong, but the eye is still teased, puzzled: Familiarity is being treated with contempt.

Watching this video you realize it is revealing a lot about *seeing*. Seeing and rhythm and motion. It is moving—moving too fast for the viewer to dissect or analyze, but not so fast as to lose you completely. The imagery fascinates the sense of sight, but defies intellectual digestion. You see the images as you hear the music—by going with them, allowing yourself, as Ong puts it, to be "incorporated." The music enhances that quality of movement, flow, the motion of emotion. As you see the video over again, you're made aware of your own constructing of what it is you see, figuring it out, the sequence, repetitions, associations, the narrative that isn't there. The question might then be asked: If young people are seeing all this as they watch videos, is anyone taking what they are learning and seeing there, and using it to teach, to show them to see other things too? It's certainly a temptation.

As another instance, take Tom Petty and the Heartbreakers' "Don't Come Around Here No More," with its intriguing appropriations of characters and imagery from Lewis Carroll's *Alice in Wonderland*. The video's set is a complex illusionistic space, a confined room of checkerboard squares, filmed from weird angles and through a fish-eye lens so that the space is persistently but irregularly distorted. A young woman dressed like Tenniel's Alice and wearing a blonde wig is seated at a large dining table. She is insistently approached by a sinister series of characters (Petty and his band) who urge her to eat, and rearrange the seating, the room, and the objects on the table to very disturbing effect. The sizes of the characters and objects alter alarmingly, without warning. The young woman is pursued around the table, and her abdomen is suddenly transformed into a birthday cake, a slice of which is cut from her side. All of which is accompanied by (or accompanies) a song entitled "Don't Come Around Here No More."

It is hard to know what this video looks like to someone who has never read Lewis Carroll's two Alice classics. But if you have, it is an oddly surrealistic treatment of those tantalizing stories, sufficiently distorted to constitute the kind of pastiche that Jameson and other theorists take to be an identifying feature of post-modernism. The chessboard, changed from red and white to black and white, has passed through some Bauhaus lens to dominate not only the room but also certain costumes; the Mad Hatter's tea party has moved indoors; Wonderland has

fallen into the Looking-Glass. Tom Petty as the Mad Hatter has gained
an entourage, excessive power, and a sinister aggression, altering in the
process his bizarre pleasure in abrupt *non sequiturs,* which generates
much of the humor in Carroll's famous scene.

Of course, by comparison with the book, the video is also very
short, a sort of crash course in the imagery of one of the most renowned
pieces of philosophical nonsense in literature. Neither the song nor the
video is much of a match for Lewis Carroll's Alice classics. But the video
is there to be reckoned with: accessible, puzzling, vivid. And at the very
least it employs a stock feature of classic literature: intertextuality. In effect it reads the song against the book. That would provide a place to
start, not just to introduce Carroll's writings and ideas, but the notion of
intertextuality itself. After all, the history of rock and roll is little else—a
limited musical vocabulary ingeniously rewritten and reinvented, marketed to an audience, half of whom recognize the references (or "rip-
offs"), and half of whom don't.

Teaching the Seen in the Scene of Teaching

All the chapters in this book acknowledge, from various points of
view but also consistently from university classroom experience, that the
very *conditions* for reading and thinking have changed, irrevocably.
Through the influence of video media, they have changed so much that
the classics which academics such as E.D. Hirsch, Allan Bloom et al.
have been energetically prescribing as indispensable for the continuation
of "cultural literacy" (that is, Civilization as 'we' know it) are in large part
opaque to their intended present-day readership. They are—literally, because literarily—dense, blank, even *incomprehensible.* When, for instance,
a student asserts that Shakespeare's *The Tempest* and Mozart's *The
Marriage of Figaro* were both written as critiques of eighteenth-century social conditions, he commits a blunder not simply out of historical ignorance, but because historical differentiation and nonsimultaneity are
structures of thinking generally suppressed in the student's own (video)
culture. To be a medium among media, then, requires either finding a
form of critical thinking that does not presuppose historical differentiation and detail, or more likely, reinstituting through video some form of
precise historical consciousness. Similar inventiveness is called for, as

most essays in this collection have indicated, in order to preserve what is critically valuable in the uncritical light of the video industries.

To put this another way, were you to begin with Tom Petty's version of Alice in "Don't Come Around Here No More" as an approach to Lewis Carroll, intertextuality, and the relationship of video to books, you would be demonstrating one of the two modes which persistently emerge in this collection as necessary responses called for by video culture: *adaptability*. You would probably be allowing for the greater attractiveness of a short, vivid, intriguing, and rather unsettling set of pictures set to music, with their very contemporary feel and technological cleverness, over the antique bookishness of Carroll's two texts. And you would be willing to find a way from one to the other (and perhaps back and forth), acknowledging the claims video has over us.

But in the process of making this maneuver, you would also find the Tom Petty tape wanting. It's too short. It has mixed up things Carroll does much more with by keeping them distinct. It (wisely) has left some of the best untouched. How it relates to the song's lyrics is rather unclear, raising questions of intent. Most of all, its treatment of Alice is decidedly unpleasant, and there is a real issue as to who the viewer identifies with, or where he or she stands in relation to the action. You would likely then be drawn to the second mode of response to video culture: *resistance*.

Indeed, adaptability and resistance are virtually the inevitable reply of any people subjected to "invasion," "occupation," "saturation," "takeover": all metaphors, Dick Hebdige observes, routinely resorted to by critics of television's impact. Devising a similarly dialectical, or shall we say ambidextrous stance towards this not-so-hidden invader is liable to be a far more convincing solution than nostalgia, lamentation, or proscription. Learn to live with your occupiers, but don't give in to them. The problem then becomes not whether this is a satisfactory policy, but how, in the face of inevitability, to devise specific means of adaption and resistance so as to make it a creative, effective basis for the inculcation of critical values.

Gregory Ulmer, in his book *Applied Grammatology: Post(e)-Pedagogy from Jacques Derrida to Joseph Beuys*, writes that

> Every teacher today, at every grade level from kindergarten to graduate school, is in a position similar to the one Socrates con-

fronted when he caught Phaedrus with the written speech concealed in his robe. The television set, the poste, is the concealed (unacknowledged) device that . . . is transforming our situation.[6]

Looking backward for a pedagogical model is only one of the possible directions for those concerned about the teaching of values in education to choose. Ulmer discusses at length a kind of post-modern educational theory that is prospective rather than retrospective. His chapter entitled "The Scene of Teaching" addresses some of the questions implicit also in our present collection: specifically, those concerning the transmission of information, the nature of inquiry and presentation, the predominance of reproduction over invention, and the antipathy toward the image within certain disciplines in the universities. Ulmer investigates older forms of pedagogy, especially the paradigm in which the teacher is "a concrete embodiment of the ideal self with which the student must identify."[7] He rejects as inadequate for the current scene the pedagogy he associates with Hegelianism, which emphasizes language as the primary "means of instruction" and "the subordination of sensation and perception to thought," both of which will ideally produce "the practical grownup who is rational and reconciled to the real."[8] Rather than arguing for a return to such methods to solve the "erosion of the humanities in a media age." Ulmer proposes a "shift away from the exclusive domination of mind . . . to a mode that includes the body."[9] He looks to Derrida, Lacan, and Beuys for exemplars of his notion of applied grammatology.

Ulmer's purpose, then, is to outline a pedagogy that provides "an educational discourse for an age of video": "Its instructional procedures are the ones appropriate for students (for a culture), whose experience of language is largely shaped by continuous exposure to cinema and television. Applied grammatology is a response to the increasing pressure the electronic media are placing on schools organized "by the book."[10]

He ends his investigation of post(e)-pedagogy with a brief survey of the theorists currently formulating ways of using audiovisual media in education. Gavriel Salomon, working with Walter Ong's theory of orality, is not, according to Ulmer, content to accept that verbal language is the only code by or through which one may extract knowledge. Somewhat similarly to Langsdorf and Hobbs, he is working on how cognition is altered as we begin to "think by means of film structuration." Genevieve Jacquinot also challenges the old theories of teaching. Her work seeks not a pedagogy dedicated to the transmission of knowledge, but an elaboration of it through an application of Barthes' readerly/writerly opposition to film. Ulmer explains, "She opposes to the traditional model a modernist, constructivist epistemology. In place of a prestructured, predigested product designed for consumption by a homogeneous group, the open pedagogy will expose the work of production, will 'make of the didactic act a process of the production of sense.'"[11]

Ulmer also directs us to *Reading Television*, by John Fiske and John Hartley, for a discussion of television as the "inner speech" of a culture, as the way a culture speaks to itself.[12] This idea was also suggested in this collection of Jeremy Murray-Brown, who gives it, however, more of a national-historical flavor.

While Gregory Ulmer is concerned that teaching should acknowledge the altered scene of post-modern reality and its discourses, Robert Scholes provides a more familiar approach to bridging the chasm between teaching texts and confronting the specter of the unreadable, television. In chapter six of this book, "Power and Pleasure in Video Texts," Scholes reads a commercial—not a rock video of a single, but a beer commercial—much as he might a text by Hemingway or Eliot. With informed historical consideration and his familiar critical acumen, he explores the amount of cultural information carried and understood by the viewer, as though it were a kind of subconscious cargo in the ad which the viewer unpacks without noticing it. Building on his understanding of the sociocultural dimensions of semiotics and his redefining of rhetoric, Scholes demonstrates how one can decipher the structures of exchange (of power and pleasure) in something as "mindless" and "contaminating" as a beer ad, by focusing on and then analyzing its textuality. He makes the ad self-conscious, by insisting on its constructedness, as well as the purposes it reveals, hides, and disguises.

Critical to his analysis is his appropriation of Eliot's notion of submission to the moment, followed by release from its power, the turning of the disenchanted critical eye. Without some moment of submission, the encounter with culture is academic, as the saying goes, clinical, statistical, disengaged. To speak to the text, be it a chapter of the Book of Judges or a video by the Book of Love, one must engage it, enter its space, go with it. One must adapt to it, and acknowledge its demands. "Language speaks us, rather than we speak it" (Gadamer again). But, Scholes argues (in accord with other literary theorists such as Gadamer and Ricoeur), one must also return to some position of independence, of other horizons, of critical distance. One must resist the text's demands for agreement, enchantment, stasis, and what Scholes designates as power, so as to speak to it. With the strength of that resistance, one may have cause to adapt again.

In his recent book *Textual Power: Literary Theory and the Teaching of English*, Scholes presents a promising pedagogical method and model, based on the teaching of texts. Its emphasis is on the student's own critical engagement—a principle which Scholes rightly sees can be extended:

> [In] the kind of textual study I am advocating[,] I have identified three aspects of such study: *reading, interpretation,* and *criticism.* Each of these can be defined by the textual activity it engenders. In *reading* we produce *text within text*; in *interpreting* we produce *text upon text*; and in *criticizing* we produce *text against text.* As teachers of literary texts we have two major responsibilities. One is to devise ways for our students to perform these productive activities as fruitfully as possible . . . : *within, upon,* and *against.* Our other responsibility is to assist students in perceiving the potent aura of codification that surrounds every verbal text. . . . Our job is *not* to intimidate students with our own superior textual production; it is to show them the codes upon which all textual production depends, and to encourage their own textual practice."[13]

It is clearly these ideas which Scholes extends in arguing that we should carefully disclose the matrices of power and pleasure in TV commercials like the "black umpire" Budweiser ad. Such an overtly textual approach may eventually prove to be problematic. But, as Moholy-Nagy once put it, "The creative possibilities of the new are mostly discovered slowly, through old forms, old instruments, old structures which are fundamentally injured by the appearance of new things but which, under the pressure of the new, emerging things, are driven up into a last, euphoric flourishing."[14] At the very least, Scholes demonstrates with his discussion of the Budweiser commercial that educators and critics concerned with discerning values should not let their distaste for popular culture or commercialism divert them from paying critical attention to powerful forms of rhetoric in our midst. To resist power one must see it, identify it, visualize it, and confront it on some common ground.

Ultimately, though, more important than reading video(s) as textual will be reversing that relation: viewing texts in the light of video('s) culture. Ultimately more important, because it will more surely anticipate the long-range consequences of the kind of revolution Murray-Brown and Alan Olson discern. And it is that more radical project that Dick Hebdige acknowledges and pursues. The challenge for thinkers and teachers is to understand print and video as complementary and interactive: to be sufficiently conversant with each set of sign-systems, and sufficiently aware of what their capabilities make possible, as well as what they hinder or obscure, to see how such coexistence might most significantly function.

The more we move towards this, the more we realize the impossibility of mastery. There are too many sign-systems to know them all, to be at home in all places. Previously distinct media, genres, icons, and value-systems are now juxtaposed and engage in transactions that are confusing but may also be sources of discovery and excitement as well as fear and misgiving. Television extends and complicates what we know already and does it very quickly, and very vividly. But print remains critical: It is much easier to bring pressure to bear on ideas in words than in images (for reasons Lenore Langsdorf has discussed at some length). If the ideal of the "cultured individual" can no longer meaningfully be registered as one who has a mastery of literate culture alone, we might more practically aim to be educated and critical in various media, across the media, able to recognize and work with the interpenetration of media, and to exploit the differences between them to reveal (or expose) their respective pleasures and powers.

One might think of this as cross-reading or *transvision*; that is, reading not just across the disciplines, but across media also, enacting in our learning and teaching this extension of textuality through multimedia. It is a way of paying attention to differences between media without penalizing the ones we don't know or like, of establishing dialogues where few have yet usefully been heard.

And attention is like unto vigilance. The "potent aura of codification" (in Scholes's phrase) that surrounds every video text—its icons, its values—needs to be brought to explicit recognition (even when the text itself is something as fleeting as the evening news). Resistance then implies an insistence that any medium and its users be kept accountable, especially in social terms. It implies teaching ourselves and youngsters to be alert to whose media it is, who owns and controls the media, why and how it is being used, and how it is using them. The capacity for critical distanciation remains crucial to true human agency within the framework of a privately owned, publicly powerful mode of mind influence, whether visual or verbal or both. We ought to be alert about who we are letting get inside our heads, and what they are doing there.

So it follows, in order to offer resistance, that one must take the video artists' lead (as David Ross indicates in his salutary essay "Truth or Consequences"[15]) and resist at the locus of influence, that is, video itself. Video art is not the only means of doing this, though it is one that educational culture could do a lot more to engage. Cues from the historical avant-garde in the visual arts would seem another very useful source for philosophers and literary critics or theorists to extend their notions of meaning. The avant-garde arts may already have been creating the means to go beyond the text-based philosophies of interpretation that have been emerging simultaneously from the legacies of Kant and Hegel. This is significant not least because implicit in the various philosophies of the avant-garde lies an essential *iconoclasm* that will neither readily submit to authority, nor accept uncritically either the powers or pleasures preferred by any master and his reason.

The chapters which comprise *Video Icons and Values* variously indicate some useful leads for undertaking such a critical engagement with video, and acknowledge certain earlier pioneering efforts. It need hardly be said that one book can scarcely even scratch the dazzling allure of the small screen. Indeed, if (as Jeremy Murray-Brown claims, and none of us sees reason to dispute) the impact of the video revolution is as colossal as that of print was earlier, any attempt to assess that revolution-in-progress must perforce be provisional, tentative, and only a small contribution to a debate which will, we trust, be as wide-ranging and open-minded as it will be perplexing and tendentious. Our collective efforts will have been successful if they persuade our readers that the conceptual and cultural transformations effected by the video revolution demand serious engagement in those intellectual areas traditionally devoted to scripture and texts, and that such a task is both possible and fruitful.

Notes

Chapter 1. Video Icons & Values.

1. See Marle Winn, *The Plug-In Drug* (New York: Bantam, 1977).

2. Rudolf Arnheim, *Visual Thinking* (Berkeley: Univ. of California Press, 1969).

3. See Hans-Georg Gadamer, *Truth and Method*, translation of 2d ed. (1965), trans. Garrett Barden and John Cumming (New York: Seabury, 1975).

4. See Neil Postman, *Amusing Ourselves to Death* (New York: Penguin, 1986).

5. See G.W.F. Hegel, *Phenomenology of Mind*, trans. J.B. Baillie (New York: Harper, 1967), pp. 558ff.

6. See Alasdair MacIntyre, *After Virtue* (Notre Dame, Ind.: University of Notre Dame Press, 1981), and *Whose Justice? Which Rationality?* (Notre Dame, Ind.: University of Notre Dame Press, 1988).

7. For a book-length treatment of this theory, see Robert Scholes's recent work, *Protocols of Reading* (New Haven, Conn.: Yale University Press, 1989).

8. See Gregor Goethals, *TV Ritual* (Boston: Beacon Press, 1982), and *Electronic Golden Calf: Images, Religion, and the Making of Meaning* (Cowley Publications, 1990).

Chapter 2. Video Ergo Sum.

1. Elizabeth L. Eisensten, *The Printing Press As An Agent of Change* (New York: Cambridge University Press, 1979), p. 44.

2. *Interfaces of the Word* (Ithaca, N.Y.: Cornell University Press, 1977), p. 316.

3. Walter J. Ong, *The Presence of the Word* (Minneapolis: University of Minnesota Press, 1981), p. 18.

4. HMSO, Cmnd 9824.

5. U.S. Department of Health and Human Services, *Television and Behavior*, Vol. 1, (1982), p. 73.

6. Ong, *Interfaces*, p. 322.

7. Nielsen Survey of 1980, quoted by Henry Scott Stokes in the *New York Times*, 22 July 1982, III, 15:1.

8. *Television and Behavior*, Vol. 2, p. 339.

9. See, inter alia, Op-Ed. article entitled "Iliterasee att Wurk" by William McGowan in the *New York Times*, 19 August 1982, page no. 19, 27:1 and Op-Ed. article by Jonathan Kozol in the *New York Times*, 30 October 1986.

10. *Books in Our Future* (U.S. Government Printing Office, 1984), p. 12.

11. Susan Sontag, *On Photography* (New York: Dell, 1982).

12. Kozol, *New York Times*, 30 October 1986.

13. Cmnd 9824, p. 78.

14. *In Search of History* (New York: Harper & Row, 1978), p. 517.

15. *Television and Behavior*, Vol. 2, p. 344.

16. Ibid., p. 342.

17. Ibid., p. 57.

18. Edward Jay Epstein, *News From Nowhere* (New York: Vintage Books, 1974), p. 242.

19. See my study of the eight KGB tapes on Andrei Sakharov and Elena Bonner, "Sakharov, The KGB and the Mass Media," undertaken for Boston University's Program for the Study of Disinformation, and published in *The New Image Makers: Soviet Propaganda and Disinformation Today*, Ladislav Bittman, ed. (McLean, Va.: Pergamon-Brassey's International Defense

Publishers, 1988), 159-200.

20. E.H. Gombrich, *The Image And The Eye* (New York: Phaidon, 1982), p. 138.

21. Epstein, p. 4.

22. Alan M. Dershowitz, *Reversal of Fortune* (New York: Random House, 1986), p. 235.

23. Epstein, p. 39.

24. "Television and Police: Attitudes and Perceptions of the Police and the Public" (New York City Police Foundation, 1987).

25. See, for example, *Crooks, Conmen and Clowns* (1981) and *Prime Time Crime* (Media Institute, 1983). See also *Television and Behavior*, passim.

26. Malcolm Muggeridge, *Christ and the Media* (Grand Rapids, Mi: Eerdmans Pub. Co., 1977), p. 59.

27. Neil Postman, *Amusing Ourselves to Death* (New York: Viking, Penguin Books, 1986), p. 77.

Chapter 3. Television and the Shaping of Cognitive Skills.

1. David Pearl, Lorraine Bouthilet, and Joyce Lazar, eds., *Television and Behavior*, Vol. 1 (Rockville, Md.: National Institute of Mental Health, 1982).

2. David R. Olson, and Jerome Bruner. "Learning Through Experience and Learning Through Media," in *Media and Symbols: The Forms of Expression, Communication and Education*, David R. Olson, ed. (Chicago: National Society for the Study of Education, 1974), 125-150.

3. Patricia Marks Greenfield, *Mind and Media*. (Cambridge: Harvard University Press, 1984).

4. W. Andrew Collins, "Schemata for Understanding Television," in *Viewing Children Through Television*. Hope Kelly and Howard Gardner, eds. (San Francisco: Jossey Bass, 1981), 31-46.

5. Gerald S. Lesser, *Children and Television* (New York: Vintage, 1974), and R. Liebert, J.M. Neale, and E.S. Davidson, *The Early Window: Effects of Television on Children and Youth*. (New York: Pergammon Press, 1973).

6. Renee Hobbs, Richard Frost, and John Stauffer, "How First-Time Viewers Comprehend Editing Conventions." *Journal of Communication*,

Autumn (1988): 50-60.

7. *The Photoplay: A Psychological Study*. (New York: Dover, 1970 [1916]).

8. Mabel Rice, Aletha Huston, and John C. Wright, "The Forms of Television: Effects on Children's Attention, Comprehension and Social Behavior," in *Children and the Formal Features of Television*, Manfred Meyer, ed. (New York: K.G. Saur Munchen, 1982).

9. Julian Hochberg, "Motion Pictures and Mental Structures." Paper presented at the Eastern Psychological Association, Washington, D.C. 1978.

10. Neil Postman, *Amusing Ourselves to Death* (New York: Viking, 1985).

11. Renee Hobbs, "Visual Verbal Synchrony and Learning from Television News." Doctoral dissertation, Harvard University, 1985.

12. *Processing the News: How People Tame the Information Tide* (New York: Longman, 1984). This quotation and the one following are both from p. 206.

13. *Harper's*, Index, August 1988.

14. Christopher H. Sterling, and John M. Kittross, *Stay Tuned: A Concise History of American Broadcasting*. (Belmont, Calif.: Wadsworth, 1978).

15. "The politics of Narrative Form: The Emergence of News Conventions in Print and Television," *Daedalus* 3, Fall (1982): 97-112.

16. Gerald Lesser, *Television and Children* (New York: Viking Press, 1974).

Chapter 4. The Emperor Has Only Clothes.

1. "Design: The Risks of Razzle-Dazzle," *New York Times*, 12 April 1987, II: 1, 34.

2. In an important sense that is easily overlooked by some who see the study of the humanities (and philosophy in particular) as destructive of traditional values, this ability to appropriate the meaning of texts is a profoundly conservative force. Demonstrating why that is so would take us away from the present topic, and so I can only suggest the line of argument by pointing out that we are more apt to be impressed by ideas and values proposed in the texts of our cultural tradition if we can entertain them on the basis of our own understanding, rather than as dogma imposed upon us. You may argue that those

goals are (at best) quaint holdovers from the Enlightenment; I counter with a defense of them as what could and even should thrive even if philosophy is dead. But that is an issue for another day.

3. I say "at most" and "typically" because some students are poor at explanatory reasoning also, while others excel in both explanatory reasoning and the sort of noncausal reasoning that I call interpretive reasoning. For a broader discussion of this difference as one of skill in "instrumental reasoning" rather than "judgment," and some causal reasoning of my own as to why students are disposed toward the former rather than the latter, see my "Is Critical Thinking a Technique, or a Means of Enlightenment?" *Informal Logic* 8 (1986): 1-17.

The strong difference I see between "explanation" and "understanding" reflects a long tradition in the history of hermeneutics. For both my understanding of that tradition and the general text theory on which I rely, I am indebted to the work of Paul Ricoeur. See, for example, his *Hermeneutics and the Human Sciences* (New York: Cambridge University Press, 1981).

It may also be helpful to acknowledge that my references to phenomenology refer primarily to the Husserlian tradition, as exemplified in the work of Robert Sokolowski and Richard Zaner. See, for example, the former's *Presence and Absence: A Philosophical Investigation of Language and Being* (Bloomington: Indiana University Press, 1978) and *Husserlian Meditations: How Words Present Things* (Evanston, Ill.: Northwestern University Press, 1974) and the latter's *The Context of Self* (Athens: Ohio University Press, 1981) and *The Way of Phenomenology* (New York: Pegasus, 1970). The hermeneutic phenomenological analysis I practice here owes much to the work of Don Ihde; see, especially, *Experimental Phenomenology* (New York: Putnam's, 1977) and *Hermeneutic Phenomenology: The Philosophy of Paul Ricoeur* (Evanston, Ill.: Northwestern University Press, 1971).

4. Examples of the sort of texts basic to those courses would be *The Apology, The Federalist Papers, Hamlet, A Tale of Two Cities, Death of a Salesman, Letter from a Birmingham Jail,* and *Under Six Flags: A History of Texas.*

5. *Oxford English Dictionary.*

6. Ontogeny recapitulates phylogeny here. That observation gives rise to speculation that one factor in our tendency to evaluate television as inferior to the printed word may be an association of video with nontechnological (natural) visual experience. We share that ability with animals and employ it from birth without any apparent effort. However, nontechnological verbal experience (i.e., speaking) develops only with some effort in humans, and is minimally or not at all present in other animals. Technologically elaborated verbal experience (i.e., handwriting and printing) share and exaggerate those "advanced," human-specific characteristics of speech. It may be that our literary proclivities encour-

age the association of video, at least from the audience point of view, with more primitive modes of experience.

An assumption underlying this analysis is that lived, verbal, and video experience are amenable to the same interpretive strategies. I follow Ricoeur here; see note 3. Also see Graeme Nicholson, *Seeing and Reading* (Atlantic Highlands, N.J.: Humanities Press, 1984); John Fiske and John Hartley, *Reading Television* (London: Methuen, 1978); and Raymond Williams, *Communications*, 3d ed. (London: Penguin, 1976).

7. Throughout this analysis the "formal features of video" are those of the contemporary commercial medium present in more than 99% of American households, and seen by the typical viewer for something in the range of 45 hours per week. Experimental and educational programming minimizes some of the formal features I identify; future technology may well, for example, provide olfactory accompaniment to the visual display. The VCR enables us to see images again, much as we can reread passages in a verbal text again. These actual and possible modifications of video do not affect this analysis, since I am concerned with the formal features of typical video at the time of this investigation.

What justifies my concern is the likelihood that this recent and pervasive technological innovation in our everyday lives is apt to affect our reasoning practices, and thus, our abilities to constitute meaning and value from our experience, more precisely, from the three modes of experience explored here. I take each of these modes as a distinct phenomenon for investigation, in the phenomenological sense of "phenomenon." Thus, to say that these formal features comprise an invariant structure for each type of experience (phenomenological domain) does not at all mean that a changed mode of experience must also exhibit them. The point is, precisely, that phenomena without these features are indeed different phenomena.

Correlatively, augmented or diminished lived experience and verbal text may fail to exemplify some of the formal features I identify here, and may exemplify others that do not appear in these examples. The lived experience chosen as example here is, precisely, one that displays a full range of sensory and cognitive possibilities. The texts at issue (those traditionally taught in humanities courses) are, precisely, examples of the sort that rely minimally on spatial-temporal structure for their meaningfulness.

8. Lest I be misunderstood: it is the lived experience of the wind that is analyzed here; no claim is made about the nature of the wind in itself, as a natural phenomenon that appears to be (presents itself as) independent of human experience. Also, in constituting that experience as meaningful, I do not understand myself as creating it or its formal structure.

In more traditional Husserlian language, the invariant formal features I identify here in all three modes of experience are "essences," and the analysis I do here is eidetic and transcendental in scope. Although I would argue that Husserl uses these terms descriptively, as I am doing here, that argument would take this exploration too far afield into phenomenological theory and methodology.

9. Research into the form of television, in contrast to the programming which is its content, is a relatively little known endeavor. The seminal writings are still those of Marshall McLuhan. Among contemporary researchers, I am most indebted to the work of Gavriel Salomon; see, e.g., his "Television is 'Easy' and Print is 'Tough': The Differential Investment of Mental Effort in Learning as a Function of Perceptions and Attributions," *Journal of Educational Psychology* 76 (1984): 647-58; *Communication and Education: Social and Psychological Interactions* (Beverly Hills: Sage, 1981); "Introducing AIME: The Assessment of Children's Mental Involvement with Television," in *Viewing Children Through Television*, H. Kelly and H. Gardner, eds. (San Francisco: Jossey Bass, 1981), pp. 89-102; *Interaction of Media, Cognition and Learning* (San Francisco: Jossey Bass, 1979).

The work of Aletha C. Huston and John C. Wright (with various colleagues) is also instrumental for the analysis I provide here. See their "Children's Understanding of the Forms of Television" in *Viewing Children Through Television*, Kelly and Gardner, eds., pp. 73-88; also "Children's Processing of Television: the Informative Functions of Formal Features," in *Children's Understanding of Television: Research on Attention and Comprehension*, J. Bryant and D.R. Anderson, eds. (New York: Academic Press, 1983), pp. 35-68; "Communicating More than Content: Formal Features of Children's Television Programs," *Journal of Communication* 31 (1981): 32-48; and "Children and Television: Effects of the Medium, its Content, and its Form," *Journal of Research and Development in Education* 13 (1979): 20-31.

A collection of papers that suggests the scope of this research is *Children and the Formal Features of Television: Approaches and Findings of Experimental and Formative Research*, M. Meyer, ed. (Munich: K.G. Saur, 1983).

Most of the formal research thus far has been concerned with children and the early development of cognitive skills. My own focus, however, has been on adults (college age and thereafter), and in connection with the problems cited in this study. More generally, I am concerned with the relationship between natural and technologically elaborated modes of knowing and communicating, on the one hand, and the relation of those to the practice of cognitive skills in everyday and academic life.

10. The "perhaps" qualifier is needed because earlier changes from oral to written experience occasioned criticism of the sort documented by Plato in his *Phaedrus*. See also Eric Havelock, *The Muse Learns to Write: Reflections on*

Orality and Literacy from Antiquity to the Present (New Haven, Conn.: Yale University Press, 1986), and *The Literate Revolution in Greece and its Consequences* (Princeton, N.J.: Princeton University Press, 1982); also, Walter Ong, *Orality and Literacy: The Technologizing of the Word* (London: Methuen, 1982).

11. This qualification, "video as a visual medium," reminds us of another difference between video and cinema. The former has been aural from its beginnings, and rarely allows silence, i.e., presentation without voice or musical background. Perhaps because of this history and perhaps also because of its limited size and inferior visual definition, video can do less visually than cinema can and seems to rely more on the formal features of spoken discourse than cinema does.

12. A listing of the main formal features of video may be helpful: compression, cuts, dissolves, dollies, ellipses, fades, flashbacks, inserts, montage, pacing, pans, switches, zooms (-in and -out).

13. For a discussion of the significance of this assessment, see Douglas Kellner's remarks on realist theories in "Television Images, Codes and Messages," *Televisions* 7 (1980): 2-19. He notes that "a critical theory of television must make clear that the television world is artificial and mediated, produced by a technical and cultural apparatus, and that it is not a 'window to the world,' a picture of reality, or a slice of life" (p. 4). Also, "Television's mimetic realism really tends toward 'pseudorealism'. . . . There are complex historical and economic reasons for the aesthetic impoverishment and restriction of codes and formulas in American television" (p. 8). This latter theme is explored further in Kellner's "Network Television and American Society: Introduction to a Critical Theory of Television," *Theory and Practice* 10 (1981): 31-62.

14. Here I am thinking of Allan Bloom's bestseller, *The Closing of the American Mind* (New York: Simon & Schuster, 1987). In a review of that work, Stuart Rosenbaum notes: "Bloom's book is an old aristocrat's lament: he mourns the loss of values and traditions that reason could not defend. What is notably missing from his book is any vision of the new democratic good that might yet be realized. . . . Vision and imagination disciplined by reason are the elements of our Socratic heritage which ultimately drive democratic culture" *Waco Tribune-Herald*, 5 July 1987: 11D. This investigation of different modes of reasoning and different forms of experience is offered as a step toward that "vision" of a "new democratic good," specifically toward considering whether and how those "values and traditions" should and could be translated into video experience.

15. Quite a few conversations have been instrumental in developing the

ideas explored here. I am especially appreciative of the insights provided by Ron Bloomquist, Jeffrey Girion, Don Ihde, Susan Lynn Peterson, Joel Rudinow, and Shea Watkins.

Chapter 5. The Electronic Golden Calf.

1. Philip Lutgendorf, "Ramayana: The Video." Unpublished paper.

2. Roger Silverstone, "Mass Communication Relies on Narrative and Myth," *Media Development*, 34 (1987): 2.

3. *Ibid.*, pp. 2-3.

4. Gloria Steinem, "Why I Consider Cagney and Lacey the Best Show On TV," *TV Guide*, 36 (16 January 1988): 5-6.

5. Alexis de Toqueville, "On the Relation Between Public Associations and the Newspaper," *Democracy in America*, vol. 2, book 2, P. Bradley, ed. (New York: Vintage Books, 1958), p. 19.

6. Gaye Tuchman, *Making News: A Study in The Construction of Reality* (New York: Free Press, 1978). See Chapters 1, 8, and 9.

7. Ronald and Nancy Reagan, "What We've Learned About America," *TV Guide* 34, (28 June 1986): 4-6.

8. "Nine Key Moments," *Time Magazine* (21 November 1988): 49.

9. Hedrick Smith, "The Power Game: Part IV," PBS documentary.

10. Mark Crispin Miller, "TV's Anti-Liberal Bias," *New York Times*, 16 November 1988, sec. 1, I, 31:1.

11. Mark Hertsgaard, *On Bended Knee: The Press and the Reagan Presidency* (New York: Farrar, Straus, and Giroux, 1988). See Chapters 14 and 15.

Chapter 6. Power and Pleasure in Video Texts.

1. See Aristotle, *The Rhetoric of Aristotle*, paragraph 1357A, Lane Cooper, ed. (New York: Appleton-Century-Crost, 1960).

2. See Frank Kermode's introduction to *Selected Prose of T.S. Eliot* (New York: Harcourt Brace Jovanovich, 1975), p. 13.

3. Mel Tormé, *The Other Side of the Rainbow* (New York: W. Morrow,

1970), p. vii.

    4. Ibid., pp. 12-15.

Chapter 7. In Video Veritas.

    1. For definitions of the icon as image, see W.J.T. Mitchell, *Iconology: Image, Text, Ideology,* (Chicago: University of Chicago Press, 1986). For definitions of the icon as myth, see *Narrative Art,* Thomas Hess and John Ashbery, eds. (New York: Macmillan, 1970).

    2. An iconic shaping vision of videography attempted here is foreshadowed by Jacques Derrida as a "painting idiom" in *The Truth of Painting* (Chicago: University of Chicago Press, 1987) and by John Bishop as a "literary idiom" in *Joyce's Book of the Dark: Finnegan's Wake* (Madison: University of Wisconsin Press, 1986). Roy Wagner in *Symbols That Stand for Themselves* (Chicago: University of Chicago Press, 1986), considers the movement of iconic meaning as an independent epistemological variable. But Gilbert J. Rose, in *Trauma and Mastery in Life and Art* (New Haven, Conn.: Yale University Press, 1987), theorizes that the movement of iconic meaning is psychologically an event dependent variable.

    3. For the best scientific description of today's "unrealistic space" see Robert Crease and Charles Mann's *The Second Creation: Makers of the Revolution in 20th Century Physics* (New York: Macmillan, 1986). Our "real time" is more creative because computer science is mythologically stronger than physics is philosophically powerful. Hence it does more for icons. See Hans Blumenberg's *Work on Myth* (Cambridge: MIT Press, 1987) for an explanation and Eric Drexler's *Engines of Creation: The Coming Era of Nanotechnology* (Garden City, N.Y.: Anchor Press, 1987) for a demonstration.

    4. Gathering or scattering? Hollis Frampton's *Circles of Confusion: Film, Photography, Video: Texts 1968-1980* (Rochester, N.Y.: Visual Studies Workshop Press, 1983) has the professional integrity to "tell it like it is." See also Yvette Biro's *Profane Mythology: The Savage Mind of the Cinema* (Bloomington: Indiana University Press, 1982). Her argument that the true originality of film is that it is not an art we can use to make sense of why the contemporary video rather than the film community is of more interest to Dürer and his descendants.

    5. I have deliberately chosen to report embryological examples that can be more fully studied in a readily available and inspiring text, namely, *Video,* Rene Payant, ed. (Montreal: Artextes, 1986). Publication of this book, partially

funded by the Canada Council, was prompted by a 1984 International Video Conference in Montreal.

6. For the first time ever, synergetic relationships between video and architecture, art, cinema, contemporary music, cuisine, dance, fashion, graphic arts, interior design, jazz, literature, media, photography, rock, and theater are studied with great depth of feeling and intellect in *Paris: Arts on the Seine*, William Mahder, ed. (Paris: Editions Autrement, 1985).

7. For a decade's record of Oriental influences on the American video community, see *Video: A Retrospective 1974-1984* (Long Beach, Calif.: Long Beach Museum of Art, 1984). We have not risen to their challenges in visual theology as well as we have in management science. See *Xerox: American Samurai* by Gary Jacobson and John Hillkirk (Collier, 1986). Nor have video installations had the cultural success of Buddhist temples. See *How the Swans Come to the Lake: A Narrative History of Buddhism in America* by Rick Fields (Boston: Shambala, 1981).

8. Rock video's phenomenal success is celebrated by Robert Pattison in *The Triumph of Vulgarity: Rock Music in the Mirror of Romanticism* (New York: Oxford University Press, 1987). In the day of Allan Bloom's *Closing of the American Mind*, is it more important than ever to "open American ears?" And when E.D. Hirsch is telling us "what every American needs to know," is it more essential than ever to determine "what every American is feeling?" Technically, *Stardust: The David Bowie Story* by Henry Edwards and Tony Zanetta (New York: McGraw-Hill, 1986), speaks well of relationships between the recording and video industries. Culturally, *Glory Days: Bruce Springsteen in the 1980's* by Dave Marsh (New York: Pantheon, 1987) speaks well of relationships between the youth culture and the video community.

9. Roland Barthes, *Mythologies* (New York: Hill and Wang, 1972), p. 143.

10. Facets of the problem of relating "undervideo" to "outertelevision" are intricately articulated by writers on images and signs and institutions in the splendid work, *Framing Feminism: Art and the Women's Movement, 1970-1985*, edited by Rozsika Parker and Griselda Pollock (London: Pandora Press, 1987).

11. Mythically, has a California oracle at last found a New England Delphi? *Whole Earth Catalog* founder, editor, and publisher Steward Brand writes on *The Media Lab: Inventing the Future at MIT* (New York: Viking, 1987).

12. From the standpoint of cultural theory we can greet this intellectual juncture with great celebration. Compare *Images of Information: Still Photography*

in *the Social Sciences*, Jon Wagner, ed. (Beverly Hills, Ca.: Sage Publications, 1979) with *New Sounds: A Listener's Guide to New Music* by John Schaefer (New York: Harper, 1987). A radical extension of the human voice is about to explode on a post-Derridean scene. Historically, music's "real time" like that of computer science is about to break the bonds of literary criticism's "unreal space" like that of physics. Behold the mystical liberation of our ancestors in *The Emancipation of Music from Language: Departure from Mimesis in Eighteenth Century Aesthetics* by John Neubauer (New Haven, Conn.: Yale University Press, 1986). For the Derrida of *Glas* to "get with it," I suggest he write in the margins of *Knowing the Score: Notes on Film Music* by Irwin Bazelon (New York: Van Nostrand Rheinhold, 1975).

13. How long, O Lord, shall we await "eye contact" between image gaining on myth and myth gaining on image? Compare the classically scientific psychological *Theories of Image Formation*, David Marks, ed. (New York: Brandon, 1986) and the engineering *Fundamentals of Imaging Systems* by William Schreiber (Cambridge: MIT Press, 1986) with the astonishing Tel Quel born-again Christianity of French feminist Julia Kristeva in *Tales of Love* (New York: Columbia University Press, 1987) and her Bengali mythical critic, Gayatri Chakravorty Spivak's *In Other Worlds: Essays in Cultural Politics* (New York: Methuen, 1987).

14. How entropy (image) comes to mathematics (myth) before physics, see Ed Regis, *Who Got Einstein's Office: Eccentricity and Genius at the Institute for Advanced Study* (New York: Addison-Wesley, 1987).

15. Questions of image gaining on myth in science fiction are ably represented by Vivian Sobchack in *Screening Space: The American Science Fiction Film* (New York: Ungar, 1987). But myth gaining on image in science fiction awaits an author as capable as Robert Eisner. We learn what formative powers of mythology we have lost to psychoanalysis in his *Road to Daulis: Psychoanalysis, Psychology, and Classical Mythology* (Syracuse, N.Y.: Syracuse University Press, 1987). We'd profit immeasurably from a sequel on parallel problems in cinematography.

16. "Icons are Microbes" possibly represents a healthy metaphor. Lynn Margulis and Dorion Sagan in *Microcosmos: Four Billion Years of Evolution from Our Microbial Ancestors* (New York: Summit Books, 1986) offer stunning vistas for video microsopy.

Chapter 8. Selling Out Max Headroom.

1. For further discussion of how cultural structures, particularly those

connected with new media, relate to dominant ideology, see Raymond Williams, *The Sociology of Culture* (New York: Schocken, 1982); Stuart Hall, "Culture, the Media and the Ideological Effect," and Theodor Adorno and Max Horkheimer, "The Culture Industry: Enlightenment as Mass Deception," in *Mass Communication and Society*, ed., James Curran, et al. (New York: Sage, 1979), pp. 349-83.

2. Edward Jay Epstein, *News from Nowhere: Television and the News* (New York: Vintage Books, 1974); Gaye Tuchman, *Making News: A Study in the Construction of Reality* (New York: Free Press, 1978).

3. See Edward Jay Epstein, *Between Fact and Fiction: The Problem of Journalism* (New York: Vintage, 1975), pp. 182-98. In 1969 ABC News was competing poorly with NBC and CBS, losing money each year largely because its affiliates would not "clear" ABC's evening news program. It therefore decided to completely redesign and restructure the evening news to increase its audience share. One major focus was the political stance which viewers perceived it taking: "After Vice President Agnew openly attacked the 'fairness' of network news, one selling point—at least to some recalcitrant affiliates—evolved that ABC would be 'fairer' in its treatment of the news than the rival networks," namely, in terms of the degree to which news coverage was favorable to the Nixon administration (p. 188). By putting one individual, Av Weston, solely in charge of the program, ABC was able to have the greatest control over the content and appearance of its news presentation.

4. Ibid., p. 192.

5. "Making the Most of Max," *Macleans*, 99 (8 December 1986): 66.

6. Harry F. Waters, with Janet Huck and Vern E. Smith, "Mad about M-M-Max," *Newsweek*, 109 (20 April 1987): 62.

7. Ibid., 59.

8. Ibid., 62.

9. Roland Barthes, "Operation Margarine," in *Mythologies*, trans. Annette Lavers (New York: Hill and Wang, 1972), p. 41.

10. Stephen Greenblatt, "Invisible Bullets: Renaissance authority and its subversion, *Henry IV* and *Henry V*," in *Political Shakespeare: New Essays in Cultural Materialism*, Jonathan Dollimore and Alan Sinfield, eds. (Ithaca, N.Y.: Cornell University Press, 1985), pp. 18-47.

11. Ronald Grover and Scott Ticer, with Jonathan Birchall, "Max Headroom is Half Human, Rude—and a Huge Hit," *Business Week* (13 October 1986): 47.

12. Waters, p. 62.

13. Waters, p. 61.

14. Adorno and Horkheimer, p. 359.

Chapter 9. What is "Soul"?

1. Jacques Attali, *Noise: The Political Economy of Music* (Ann Arbor: University of Minnesota, 1985), p. 3.

2. Walter J. Ong, *Orality and Literacy: The Technologizing of the Word* (New York: Methuen, 1985), p. 32.

3. Ibid., p. 72.

4. Attali, p. 11.

5. Gaston Bachelard, The Poetics of Space (Boston: Beacon Press, 1969), p. 46. The Charles Nodier quotation is from *Dictionnaire raisonné des onomatopées francaises* (Paris, 1928), quoted by Bachelard, p. xvi.

6. Paul Gilroy, *There Ain't No Black in the Union Jack* (London: Hutchison, 1987), p. 235.

7. Larry Grossberg, "The Politics of Youth Culture: Some Observations on Rock and Roll in American Culture," *Social Text* Winter 8 (1983): 104-126.

Chapter 10. An Afterword: Beyond Lamentation.

1. Dick Hebdige, "Post-script 4: Learning to Live on the Road to Nowhere," *Hiding in the Light: On Images and Things* (New York: Routledge, 1988), pp. 233-44.

2. Ibid., p. 239.

3. Ibid., p. 240.

4. Dick Hebdige, from the unpublished manuscript score of the lecture-presentation "What Is 'Soul'?"

5. Ibid.

6. Gregory Ulmer, *Applied Grammatology: Post(e)-Pedagogy from Jacques Derrida to Joseph Beuys* (Baltimore, Md.: Johns Hopkins University Press, 1985), p. 301. The reader's attention is also drawn to Ulmer's *Teletheory* (New

York: Routledge, 1989), which unfortunately appeared too late for us to refer to.

7. *Applied Grammatology*, p. 166.

8. Ibid., p. 166-7.

9. Ibid., p. 164, 168.

10. Ibid., p. 265.

11. Ibid., p. 307.

12. Ibid., p. 332.

13. Robert Scholes, *Textual Power: Literary Theory and the Teaching of English* (New Haven, Conn.: Yale University Press, 1985), p. 24.

14. Walter Benjamin, "A Short History of Photography." Reprinted in *Classic Essays on Photography*, Alan Trachtenberg, ed. (New Haven, Conn.: Leete's Island Books, 1980), pp. 199-216. This quotation is from p. 212.

15. David Ross, "Truth or Consequences: American Television and Video Art," in *Video Culture: A Critical Investigation*, John Hanhardt, ed. (Layton, Utah: Peregrine Smith Books, 1986), pp. 167-78. For a wide-ranging consideration of various applications of video to the presentation of diverse art-forms, see the excellent catalogue *The Arts for Television*, Kathy Rae Huffman and Dorine Mignot, eds. (Los Angeles: MOCA, and Amsterdam: Stedelijk Museum, 1987). This includes an essay by Rosetta Brooks on "Music for Television."

Selected Bibliography

Adler, Richard P., ed. *Understanding Television: Essays on Television as a Social and Cultural Force*. New York: Praeger, 1981.

Allen, R. *Channels of Discourse: Television and Contemporary Criticism*. Chapel Hill: University of North Carolina Press, 1987.

Attali, Jacques. *Noise: The Political Economy of Music*. Minneapolis: University of Minnesota, 1985.

Bachelard, Gaston. *The Poetics of Space*. Trans. Maria Jolas. Boston: Beacon Press, 1969.

Barthes, Roland. *Mythologies*. Trans. Annette Lavers. New York: Hill and Wang, 1972.

Baudrillard, Jean. *Simulations*. Trans. Paul Foss, Paul Patton, and Philip Beitchman. New York: Semiotext(e), 1983.

Benjamin, Walter. "A Short History of Photography." Reprinted in *Classic Essays on Photography*. Alan Trachtenberg, ed. (pp. 199-216). New Haven, Conn.: Leete's Island Books, 1980.

Berger, Arthur Asa, ed. *Television in Society*. New Brunswick, N.J.: Transaction Books, 1987.

Biro, Yvette. *Profane Mythology: The Savage Mind of the Cinema*. Bloomington: Indiana University Press, 1982.

Bittman, Ladislav [Lawrence Martin]. *The New Image-Makers: Soviet Propaganda and Disinformation Today.* McLean, Va.: Pergamon-Brassey's International Defense Publishers, 1988.

Bloom, Allan. *The Closing of the American Mind.* New York: Simon & Schuster, 1987.

Blumenberg, Hans. *Work on Myth.* Cambridge: MIT Press, 1987.

Brand, Stewart. *The Media Lab: Inventing the Future at MIT.* New York: Viking, 1987.

Bryant, J., and D.R. Anderson, eds. *Children's Understanding of Television: Research on Attention and Comprehension.* New York: Academic Press, 1983.

Burns, Gary, and Robert J. Thompson, eds. *Television Studies: Textual Analysis.* New York: Praeger, 1989.

Cohen, S., and J. Young. *The Manufacture of the News: Deviance, Social Problems, and the Mass Media.* London: Constable, 1973.

Curran, James, et al., eds. *Mass Communication and Society.* New York: Sage, 1979.

Derrida, Jacques. *The Truth in Painting.* Chicago: University of Chicago Press, 1987.

Drexler, Eric. *Engines of Creation: The Coming Era of Nanotechnology.* Garden City, N.Y.: Anchor, 1987.

Edwards, Henry, and Tony Zanetta. *Stardust: The David Bowie Story.* New York: McGraw-Hill, 1986.

Eisenstein, Elizabeth L. *The Printing Press As An Agent of Change.* Cambridge: Cambridge University Press, 1979.

Epstein, Edward Jay. *Between Fact and Fiction: The Problem of Journalism.* New York: Vintage, 1975.

———. *News from Nowhere: Television and the News.* New York: Vintage, 1974.

Fiske, John. *Television Culture.* London: Methuen, 1987.

Fiske, John, and John Hartley. *Reading Television.* London: Methuen, 1978.

Foster, Hal. *The Anti-Aesthetic: Essays in Postmodern Culture.* Port Townsend, Wash.: Bay Press, 1983.

Frampton, Hollis. *Circles of Confusion: Film, Photography, Video: Texts 1968-*

1980. Rochester, N.Y.: Visual Studies Workshop Press, 1983.

Frith, Simon. *The Sociology of Rock*, rev. ed. London: Constable, 1984.

Gilroy, Paul. *There Ain't No Black in the Union Jack.* London: Hutchison, 1987.

Goethals, Gregor. *The Electronic Golden Calf: Images, Religion, and the Making of Meaning.* Cambridge, Mass.: Cowley Publications, 1990.

———. *The TV Ritual: Worship at the Video Altar.* Boston: Beacon Press, 1981.

Gombrich, E.H. *The Image And The Eye.* New York: Phaidon, 1982.

Graber, Doris. *Processing the News: How People Tame the Information Tide.* New York: Longman, 1984.

Greenfield, Patricia Marks. *Mind and Media.* Cambridge: Harvard University Press, 1984.

Grossberg, Larry. "The Politics of Youth Culture: Some Observations on Rock and Roll in American Culture." *Social Text* Winter 8 (1983): 104-126.

Hall, Stuart, J. Clarke, T. Jefferson, and B. Roberts, eds. *Resistance Through Rituals.* London: Hutchinson, 1976.

Hall, Stuart, and Paddy Whannel. *The Popular Arts.* New York: Pantheon, 1965.

Havelock, Eric. *The Literate Revolution in Greece and Its Consequences.* Princeton, N.J.: Princeton University Press, 1982.

———. *The Muse Learns to Write: Reflections on Orality and Literacy from Antiquity to the Present.* New Haven, Conn.: Yale, 1986.

Hanhardt, John, ed. *Video Culture: A Critical Investigation.* Layton, Utah: Peregrine Smith Books, 1986.

Hebdige, Dick. *Hiding in the Light: On Images and Things.* New York: Routledge, 1988.

———. Subculture: *The Meaning of Style.* London: Methuen, 1979.

Hess, Thomas, and John Ashbery, eds. *Narrative Art.* New York: Macmillan, 1970.

Hirsch, E.D., Jr. *Cultural Literacy: What Every American Needs to Know.* New York: Vintage, 1988.

Hobbs, Renee, Richard Frost, and John Stauffer. "How First-Time Viewers Comprehend Editing Conventions." *Journal of Communication,*

Autumn 1988: Vol. 38 (4), 50-60.

Huffman, Kathy Rae. *Video: A Retrospective 1974-1984*. Long Beach: Long Beach Museum of Art, 1984.

————, and Dorine Mignot, eds. *The Arts for Television*. Los Angeles: MOCA, and Amsterdam: Stedelijk Museum, 1987.

Huston, Aletha C., and John C. Wright. "Children and Television: Effects of the Medium, its Content, and its Form," *Journal of Research and Development in Education* 13 (1979): 20-31.

————. "Communicating More than Content: Formal Features of Children's Television Programs," *Journal of Communication* 31 (1981): 32-48.

Ihde, Don. *Experimental Phenomenology*. New York: Putnam's, 1977.

————. *Hermeneutic Phenomenology: The Philosophy of Paul Ricoeur*. Evanston, Ill.: Northwestern University Press, 1971.

Journal of Communication Inquiry. MTV issue. 10 (Winter 1986).

Journal of Communication. 36 (Winter 1986).

Kaplan, E. Ann. *Rocking Around The Clock: Music Television, Postmodernism, and Consumer Culture*. New York: Methuen, 1987.

————. ed. *Regarding Television: Critical Approaches—An Anthology*. Los Angeles: American Film Institute/University Publications of America, 1983.

Kellner, Douglas. "Network Television and American Society: Introduction to a Critical Theory of Television," *Theory and Practice* 10 (1981): 31-62.

————. "Television Images, Codes and Messages," *Televisions* 7 (1980): 2-19.

Kelly, Hope, and Howard Gardner, eds. *Viewing Children Through Television*. San Francisco, Calif.: Jossey Bass, 1981 .

Kottak, C.P. *Prime-Time Society: An Anthropological Analysis of Television and Culture*. Belmont, Calif.: Wadsworth, 1990.

Kristeva, Julia. *Tales of Love*. New York: Columbia University Press, 1987.

Langsdorf, Lenore. "Is Critical Thinking a Technique, or a Means of Enlightenment?" *Informal Logic* 8 (1986): 1-17.

Lesser, Gerald S. *Children and Television*. New York: Vintage, 1974.

Levy, Stephen. "Ad Nauseam—How MTV Sells Out Rock and Roll." *Rolling Stone* 8 December 1983: 30-31.

Liebert, R., J.M. Neale, and E.S. Davidson. *The Early Window: Effects of Television on Children and Youth*. New York: Pergamon, 1973.

McCabe, Colin. *High Theory/Low Culture: Analysing Popular Television and Film*. Manchester: Manchester University Press, 1986.

McLuhan, Marshall. *The Gutenberg Galaxy: The Making of Typographic Man*. Toronto: University of Toronto Press, 1962.

———. *Understanding Media: The Extensions of Man*. New York: McGraw-Hill, 1964.

———, and Quentin Fiore. *The Medium is the Massage*. New York: Bantam Books, 1967.

Mahder, William, ed. *Paris: Arts on the Seine*. Paris: Editions Autrement, 1985.

Mander, Jerry. *Four Arguments For The Elimination of Television*. New York: Morrow, 1978.

Marcus, Greil. *Mystery Train: Images of America in Rock 'n' Roll Music*. Rev. ed. New York: Dutton, 1985.

Marks, Edward, ed. *Theories of Image Formation*. New York: Brandon, 1986.

Marsh, Dave. *Glory Days: Bruce Springsteen in the 1980s*. New York: Pantheon, 1987.

Meyer, Manfred, ed. *Children and the Formal Features of Television: Approaches and Findings of Experimental and Formative Research*. Munich: K.G. Saur, 1983.

Miller, Mark Crispin. *Boxed In: The Culture of TV*. Evanston, Ill.: Northwestern University Press, 1988.

Mitchell, W.J.T. *Iconology: Image, Text, Ideology*. Chicago: University of Chicago Press, 1986.

Modleski, Tania, ed. *Studies in Entertainment: Critical Approaches to Mass Culture*. Bloomington: Indiana University Press, 1986.

Muggeridge, Malcolm. *Christ and the Media*. Grand Rapids, Mich.: Eerdmans, 1977.

Munsterberg, Hugo. *The Photoplay: A Psychological Study*. New York: Dover, [1916], 1970.

Neubauer, John. *The Emancipation of Music from Language: Departure from Mimesis in Eighteenth Century Aesthetics*. New Haven, Conn.: Yale University Press, 1986.

Nicholson, Graeme. *Seeing and Reading*. Atlantic Highlands, N.J.: Humanities Press, 1984.

Olson, David R., ed. *Media and Symbols: The Forms of Expression, Communication and Education*, Chicago: National Society for the Study of Education, 1974.

Ong, Walter J. *Interfaces of the Word*. Ithaca, N.Y.: Cornell University Press, 1977.

————. *Orality and Literacy: The Technologizing of the Word*. New York: Methuen, 1985.

————. *The Presence of the Word*. Minneapolis: University of Minnesota Press, 1981.

Orman, John. *The Politics of Rock Music*. Chicago: Nelson-Hall, 1984.

Pattison, Robert. *The Triumph of Vulgarity: Rock Music in the Mirror of Romanticism*. New York: Oxford University Press, 1987.

Parker, Rozsika, and Griselda Pollock, eds. *Framing Feminism: Art and the Women's Movement, 1970-1985*. London: Pandora Press, 1987.

Payant, Rene, ed. *Video*. Montreal: Artextes, 1986.

Pearl, David, Lorraine Bouthilet, and Joyce Lazar, eds. *Television and Behavior*. Rockville, Md.: National Institute of Mental Health, 1982.

Postman, Neil. *Amusing Ourselves to Death*. New York: Viking, 1985.

Ricoeur, Paul. *Hermeneutics and the Human Sciences*. Cambridge: Cambridge University Press, 1981.

Rose, Gilbert J. *Trauma and Mastery in Life and Art*. New Haven, Conn.: Yale University Press, 1987.

Rowland, Willard D. Jr., and Bruce Watkins, eds. *Interpreting Television: Current Research Perspectives*. Beverly Hills, Calif.: Sage, 1984.

Salomon, Gavriel. *Communication and Education: Social and Psychological Interactions*. Beverly Hills, Calif.: Sage, 1981.

————. *Interaction of Media, Cognition and Learning*. San Francisco, Calif.: Jossey Bass, 1979.

————. "Television is 'Easy' and Print is 'Tough': The Differential Investment of Mental Effort in Learning as a Function of Perceptions and Attributions," *Journal of Educational Psychology*. 76 (1984): 647-58.

Schaefer, John. *New Sounds: A Listener's Guide to New Music*. New York: Harper, 1987.

Scholes, Robert. *Protocols of Reading*. New Haven, Conn.: Yale University Press, 1989.

———. *Textual Power: Literary Theory and the Teaching of English*. New Haven, Conn.: Yale University Press, 1985.

Schneider, Cynthia, and Brian Wallis, eds. *Global Television*. New York: Wedge Press, 1988.

Schreiber, William. *Fundamentals of Imaging Systems*. Cambridge: MIT Press, 1986.

Schudson, Michael. "The Politics of Narrative Form: The Emergence of News Conventions in Print and Television," *Daedalus* 3 (1982): 97-112.

Sobchack, Vivian. *Screening Space: The American Science Fiction Film*. New York: Ungar, 1987.

Sokolowski, Robert. *Husserlian Meditations: How Words Present Things*. Evanston, Ill.: Northwestern University Press, 1974.

———. *Presence and Absence: A Philosophical Investigation of Language and Being*. Bloomington: Indiana University Press, 1978.

Sontag, Susan. *On Photography*. New York: Dell, 1982.

Spivak, Gayatri Chakravorty. *In Other Worlds: Essays in Cultural Politics*. New York: Methuen, 1987.

Sterling, Christopher H., and John M. Kittross. *Stay Tuned: A Concise History of American Broadcasting*. Belmont, Calif.: Wadsworth, 1978.

Trachtenberg, Alan, ed. *Classic Essays on Photography*. New Haven, Conn.: Leete's Island Books, 1980.

Tuchman, Gaye. *Making News: A Study in the Construction of Reality*. New York: Free Press, 1978.

Ulmer, Gregory. *Applied Grammatology: Post(e)-Pedagogy from Jacques Derrida to Joseph Beuys*. Baltimore, Md.: Johns Hopkins University Press, 1985.

———. *Teletheory*. New York: Routledge, 1989.

Wagner, Jon, ed. *Images of Information: Still Photography in the Social Sciences*. Beverly Hills, Calif.: Sage Publications, 1979.

Wagner, Roy. *Symbols That Stand for Themselves*. Chicago: Chicago University

Press, 1986.

Waites, B., T. Bennet, and G. Martin, eds. *Popular Culture: Past and Present.* London: Open University Press, 1982.

Waters, Harry F., with Janet Huck and Vern E. Smith, "Mad about M-M-Max," *Newsweek.* 109 (20 April 1987): 62.

White, Theodore H. *In Search of History: A Personal Adventure.* New York: Harper & Row, 1978.

Williams, Raymond. *Communications.* 3d ed. London: Penguin Books, 1976.

————. *The Sociology of Culture.* New York: Schocken, 1982.

————. *Television: Technology and Cultural Form.* New York: Schocken, 1975.

ner, Richard. *The Context of Self.* Athens, Ohio: Ohio University Press, 1981.

————. *The Way of Phenomenology.* New York: Pegasus, 1970.

Contributors

Rebecca L. Abbott teaches Media Studies at Sacred Heart University in Fairfield, Connecticut. Her work as a filmmaker has been shown on Connecticut Public Television and at various screenings in New York, Los Angeles, and Chicago.

Gregor Goethals writes on mass-mediated culture from the perspectives of an art historian and practicing artist. She is professor of Art History at the Rhode Island School of Design, Providence, Rhode Island. She is author of *The TV Ritual* and *The Electronic Golden Calf: Images, Religion, and the Making of Meaning*, from which she has distilled concepts and selected symbols of authority for this paper.

Dick Hebdige is a lecturer in the Department of Communications, Goldsmith College, University of London. His many publications include: *Subculture: The Meaning of Style*, *Cut 'n' Mix*, and most recently, *Hiding in the Light: On Images and Things*.

Renee Hobbs is an assistant professor of Communication at Babson College in Wellesley, Massachusetts. She has an extensive research background at Project Zero, the Center for Research on Children's Television, and the Media and Social Science Project at Harvard University.

Lenore Langsdorf is associate professor in the Philosophy of Communication Group of the Speech Communication Department at Southern Illinois University, Carbondale. Her primary areas of research are the phenomenology of communication, sociopolitical philosophy, and argumentation theory.

Jeremy Murray-Brown is an associate professor of Broadcasting in the School of Communication at Boston University. He has an extensive background with the BBC including the series *A Third Testament* with Malcolm Muggeridge, which he directed and edited.

Alan M. Olson is an associate professor of Religion and the chairman, *ad interim*, of the Department of Philosophy at Boston University. His forthcoming book is *Hegel and the Spirit: Philosophy as Pneumatology*.

Christopher Parr is a New Zealander presently completing his doctoral dissertation in religion and literature at Boston University. He has worked in music management, written for music and arts magazines, and has held various positions, including curatorial assistant for video, at the Institute of Contemporary Art, Boston.

Debra Parr is presently completing her doctoral dissertation on modern and postmodern American landscapes, in the Department of English at Boston University. Her areas of teaching and literary research include avant-garde and multimedia treatments of representation.

Robert Scholes is professor of English and Comparative Literature at Brown University. A major semiotician and anthologist, his many writings include: *Semiotics and Interpretation, Elements of Fiction: An Anthology, Textual Power* and *Protocols of Reading*.

E. David Thorp recently received his Ph.D. in the History of Consciousness program at the University of California, Santa Cruz, where he has served as a teaching fellow in Stevenson College. He is the author of the forthcoming book *Arts and Sciences for Videography: Perception and Myth; Image and Intervention*.

Index

175